Art in movement

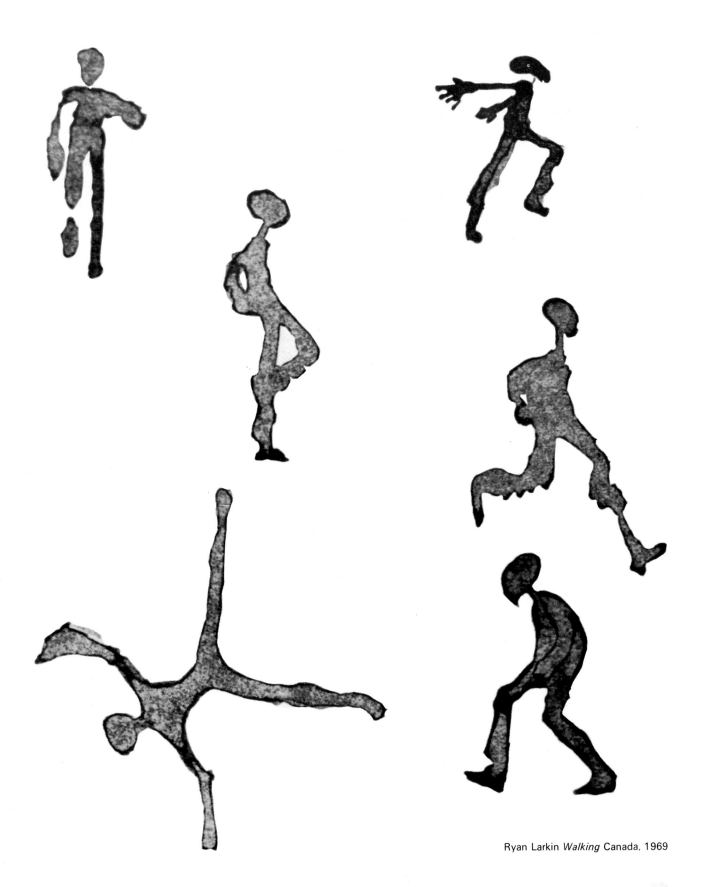

Ryan Larkin *Walking* Canada, 1969

Art in movement:
new directions in animation

by JOHN HALAS
in collaboration with Roger Manvell

Visual Communication Books

Hastings House, Publishers
10 East 40th Street, New York 10016

Acknowledgements

I would like to express my sincere gratitude to Dr Roger Manvell, who has spent so much time helping me with the text of this book.

I also wish to thank my colleagues from all over the world, the members of ASIFA, BBC Television, Granada Television, The National Film Board of Canada, NZBC Television and Zagreb Film who kindly submitted their work for selection.

John Halas 1970

Cover: drawings by Pavle Stalter *Mask of the Red Death* Yugoslavia, 1969-70

Contents

1 The kinetic link: art and movement

The film is an art of disciplined movement. It is entirely dependent on technology which it uses to fulfill the complex needs of contemporary expression through art, either by means of live cinematography or, more exactingly, animation. Animation is at its purest in the art of mobile graphics.

Movement is the sign of all living organisms. The human species, animals, plants, all living organisms, from the smallest microplasms to the largest cells, manifest their existence through movement. It is their essential characteristic from the moment of conception to death and final decay. At the opposite extreme in scale we are increasingly trying to come to terms with colossal forms of movement which are almost beyond our capacity to conceive or imagine. The universe, whether interpreted in origin and development as 'steady state' or 'big bang', involves ceaseless movement. The Einstein and post-Einstein theory of relativity depends upon relationships made up of time and energy in motion. Nothing, in fact, within any kind or scale of existence known to us is still. Even sound and light, on which we depend if we are to apprehend the universe, are themselves forms of energy in motion.

Science has been able to analyse, to measure and to exploit physical energy to a great extent during the last decades. The conversion of energy by splitting the hydrogen atom led to the nuclear explosion; the concentration of light energy into a narrow channel led to the laser beam and to holography; the utilization of electricity led to the computer. In every case forms of dynamic movement are involved. It would be difficult for the artist not to be influenced by such discoveries when they lead to exciting experiments. As a source of inspiration, movement can be classified in the following general terms:

Physical forces:

gravity; wind; tide; electricity; magnetism.

Organic or biological forces:

life cycle in humans, animals and plants.

Kinetic art utilizes gravity, electricity, imagination. The stage utilizes human motion in the forms of ballet and mime. Film attempts to utilize them all. But both stage and film are primarily concerned with literary drama and little consideration is given to the use of motion mechanics for its own sake. It is left to kinetic art to interpret movement creatively, and to film animation to do the same in the optical field. Both are the purest form of expression to convey motion mechanics, and in this area they are closely related.

The artist is largely responding to the nature of the movement itself. Such responses as these have led in our century to certain forms of kinetic art, a branch of graphic and three-dimensional art which is developing rapidly in many directions and which has excited, at least in its simpler forms, considerable popular favour. Kinetic art has become a recognized part of contemporary culture, part of our so-called technological age. The concepts and activities of science and technology are a primary source of enrichment for the visual imagery of the artist.

Kinetic art offers an obvious bridge between graphic art and film. Frank Popper, in his book *Origins and Development of Kinetic Art,* traces movement as a source of inspiration for the artist as far back as the eighteenth century. From the point of view of the film-maker, practising an art form which dates back only to the 1890s, the medium of cinema (a word derived from the Greek word, *kinema,* meaning 'movement') inspires by its very nature an increasing, developing concentration on the potentialities of movement as a powerful component within the disciplines of film art.

Just as kinetic art is in itself a pure form, which relies solely on exploiting certain disciplines of movement and is free from any other ostensible 'content' or 'meaning', so experimental animation could become the purest form of film art, exploiting 'abstract' mobile forms. Certain film-makers have drawn or painted direct on to the celluloid (Hans Richter, Viking Eggeling, Len Lye, Norman McLaren, and many others) without any kind of intermediate photography at all—they have created their kinetic art by exploiting the rapid movement of the reel of celluloid through the projector, adding a mechanized dynamic to the continuity of their 'still' graphics. This kind of animated film-making is an extension of those forms of kinetic art which employ simple mechanisms to rotate or give other repetitive forms of movement to their work. The basic difference between the activity of pure kinetic art and film is that the first creates actual movement through animating real objects and constructions (video-rotors, rotating works, sculptural mobiles, light paintings, etc.), while the second achieves its effects through the mechanisms of cinematography and cineprojection. Cinematography still depends on a number of separate stages to achieve its final effects. Photography, processing, editing and projection are steps through which the end results emerge. It can, however, exploit creatively some of its own mechanical processes, as well as newer inventions in machine technology. For instance, the exploitation of the speed of the projector (24 frames per second in 35 millimetres) led to artists painting directly on to the film stock itself, which established the abstract cinema. This also meant that movement could be synchronized to music to the utmost perfection. When oscilloscopes came into use and revealed sound waves visually on to the cathode ray tube, it was soon utilized for stereoscopic animation. The latest device, the computer, is also gradually being exploited for a variety of forms of animation, from simple lively movement to more complex textural changes. This is art 'processed' mechanically, a new concept which requires new, contemporary responses both from the creative artist and the spectator.

During the earlier periods of the twentieth century, both film and kinetic art were developing from their own embryonic forms, mostly quite separately, but on occasion together. In the case of the cinema, Emile Cohl and George Méliès completed their principal experimental work between 1904 and 1914—Cohl in 'matchstick' animation, Méliès in fantasies which, though performed in live action, introduced many newly discovered cinematic devices of trick photography and special effects. Even before the cinema had come into existence, advanced forms of magic-lantern projection had developed elementary forms of motion which anticipated animation—for example, in the case of Marey's flow of graphic images. Later, in the 1920s, the realization of the potentialities of film art increased, especially in the avant-garde cinema of France and Germany: some artists 'adopted' the film in order to achieve their own special, abstract, or semi-abstract continuities and Fernand Léger made *Le Ballet Mécanique* (1924), exploiting special cinephotographic effects and the devices of dynamic *montage* fashionable at this time. In America Robert Florey made *The Love of Zero* (1923), including mobile abstracts of machines; in France, Eugen Deslav was responsible for *Marche des Machines* (1928), another visual interpretation of a mechanical age with abstract images; while in Britain a little later, Francis Bruguière and Oswell Blakeston played moving lights on cardboard cut-out mobiles in *Light Rhythms* (1931), and Laszlo Moholy-Nagy created the celebrated mobile abstract sequence for the film made from H. G. Wells's script, *Things to Come* (1935).

The movement, however, was two-way; the influences of the cinema were reflected both consciously and unconsciously in other forms of art. Gordon Craig, for example, became involved when he planned his special art of movement in *Scene* (1923), in which he proposed his own form of stage dynamic in the theatre by projecting moving light on mobile scenic devices: this, too, was a form of kinetics, or the creative representation of pure movement. Léger also used lighting effects and mobile objects for his stage productions; the principles demonstrated in *Le Ballet Mécanique* were similar to those he adopted in his décor for the ballets *La Patinoire* and *Le Fin du Monde*.

The influence of cinematographic principle has also been much in evidence in static paintings. Balla's *Automobile and Noise* (1912), *Racing Automobile* (1913) and *Flight of Swallows* (1913) for instance, radiate with movement. Dottori, Marc and Boccioni, the leaders of the futurist movement during the first part of this century, as well as Léger, packed so powerful an illusion of motion on to their canvasses that they virtually explode with energy. The desire to represent motion was very much in evidence even if attempted through an artificial means. But in the case of Léger and Duchamp the abstract rhythm was achieved in two dimensions which had to be followed by the added dimension of time and space. The logical conclusion to this problem was to experiment with the motion-picture camera which was able to provide movement in three dimensions through the medium of film, and could manipulate time by speeding or slowing down an action.

The significance of the work of Marcel Duchamp in this context is obvious. Duchamp wrote: 'A picture is not a painting, but an organization of kinetic elements—an expression of time and space through the abstract presentation of movement'. Not only was his work outstanding in the development of kinetic art, he also understood the potentialities of the cinema and produced a film with Man Ray and Marc Allegret called *Anaemic Cinema* (1928), in which a succession of rotating drawings on discs were interspersed with rotating, spiralling inscriptions designed by Duchamp. His *Rotative Demi-Spheres* (1925) and *Disques Visuels* (1932) were among the first works to create an illusion of three-dimensional movement, though the work of the artists at the Bauhaus in Germany, particularly under the influence of Moholy-Nagy, had by 1924 experimented with space, light and movement, exploring the visual potentialities of newly developed materials in plastic and metal, and created dynamic relationships by allying natural forces (gravity, wind and so forth), with mechanically controlled movement.

Artists like Victor Vasarely are currently experimenting with 'kinetic' animation through static painting. His canvasses attempt to convey an optical study of movement. Some are painted on transparent screens which are arranged in depth in front of coloured surfaces, the onlooker providing the animation. An interesting line of development has been pursued by Takis in exploring magnetism in his kinetic mobiles *Signals* and *Telesculpture*. He is attempting to reveal the natural forces which exist invisibly in steel, in iron, and in other metals when magnetism and gravity act upon them.

An outstanding kinetic artist is Nicholas Schöffer, who introduces the cinematographic element of projection by providing light and movement on the screen with kinetic moving structures. The structures (all sculptural constructions), are driven by hidden motors and their motion is synchronized with what can be called 'visual music'. These mobiles replace old-fashioned sculptures and are used as novel spectacles in places like the Central Station, New York. Lately he has extended his technique staging 'Son et Lumière' spectacles with certain abstract light effects.

Another artist to note is Jean Tinguely, who believes that the machines he constructs are living beings, generating a wide range of emotions. He is one of the few kinetic artists with a distinct sense of humour. His humour lies in the construction of his machines and their mechanical movements accompanied by sound effects of machine noises.

The motion paintings of Peter Sedgley, Jeffrey Steele and John Healey depend on micro-motors driving colour plates which are projected as colour light effects on to the canvas.

There is no doubt that the new materials and micro-motors introduced during recent years have had a stimulating effect on kinetic art and helped to make it once again internationally fashionable. The new techniques, such as employing sound and projected light, have drawn it even nearer to animation. In the meantime it appears that the challenge which kinetic art can offer draws the young artist away from the traditional practice of drawing and painting on flat surfaces. This also applies to film arts which have been developing and expanding both technically and artistically during the last decades. During that period cinema has moved closer to kinetic art in many of its new manifestations. One of them, the Magic Lantern system, combines stage performance with live actors and film projection in three dimensions. The significance of this performance was the use of movement through space and with time, the basis of kinetics, and an important element in all contemporary visual experiments.

During the 1950s the first imaginative development of three-dimensional form was seen, notably in the abstract mobility of Norman McLaren's experimental film *Around is Around* (1951). Film became an integrated element in other forms of representation as well—in the system known as the Living Screen (1964), for example, live performers interact with their own images on the screen.

Forms of cinema have evolved which merge the audience with the screen image, giving them a direct physical experience of involvement in the projection. This began with the three-dimensional film, and also with the illusion created by the original deeply curved screen of Cinerama (1952), which, when viewed from a relatively close, central position in the theatre, appeared to 'absorb' the spectator into the 'environment' of the action. Cinema-in-the-round developed soon after, the spectator standing inside a circular theatre completely surrounded by a synchronized series of images which collectively give an all-round view of the scene and action, the viewer turning at will to look, as in real life, either in front or behind. As in the kinetic arts, the boundaries of the film medium have loosened, integrating film with many other forms of spectacle, just as theatrical and pageant spectacle has diversified, for example, in theatre-in-the-round or displays of Son et Lumière. From the point of view of the audience, many of these new spectacles with their various degrees of physical involvement, offer an entirely new form of audience participation or experience.

Animation, although a small part of the total structure of the film industry, is a medium which is creating new ideas and styles, and seeking out-of-the-way forms to a far greater extent than other forms of film-making or the living theatre. Because of its flexibility of technique, and the fact that the artist is still in full control through his individual contact with the medium, it is a more immediate form in which to carry out creative experiment. Since the creation of motion—whether achieved through frame-by-frame progression, camera mobility, or the manipulation of light effects—is the essence of animation, it is the pure form of art which comes closest to the kinetic movement. The fact that film mobiles in the form of animation require a screen and projection for their presentation does not affect their reliance for their creativity on motion mechanics. The fact that animation can be employed for highly commercial purposes in advertising, industry and for technical purposes in education, does not alter its basic affiliation to kinetics. Animation provides the link between the newly developed kinetics in art—which also started to use such physical factors as gravity, electricity and mobile lighting effects—and the contemporary cinema. Through animation, the cinema has added to the use of these physical factors a freer and wider range of creative work embodying the principles of optics employed within an increasing variety of screen ratios and formats.

Rotareliefs (Optical Discs)
(France, 1935)

An early example of the application of kinetic principles, with cinematographic effects achieved by simple means. Duchamp used the same principle when he worked with Hans Richter in the mid-1950s on Richter's colour film *Dreams that Money Can Buy.*

CARMEN D'AVINO

The Wall
(USA, 1970)

The Wall is a short section from a film of feature length. It was filmed initially using normal, live-action camera coverage of a multiplicity of objects.

The camera panned over the surface of these objects, occasionally coming to rest on some particular one. Many of the objects were chosen because they had some direct relationship to d'Avino's past life; since his recollections cover a period of fifty years he was able to draw on a multitude of different objects for the film. The wall itself is used as a device to get from one moment in time to another; it also takes on a life of its own when it is being covered with paint. Various objects are overwhelmed by the onrushing colours.

14

COLIN HOEDEMAN

La Boule Magique
(Canada, 1969)

The National Film Board of Canada (French section) in Montreal is an establishment where many interesting experiments have been carried out in motion cinematography. Colin Hoedeman, for instance, has been able to create a fluid movement by using plastic wires and advancing the action frame by frame.

FRED MOGUBGUB

Sky Rings of the Mind
(USA, 1970)

This film, which has three stages of development, was started in the Spring of 1968, and its visuals completed a year later. The film should be finished in the Spring of 1971. According to notes supplied by Fred Mogubgub, the film originated in the title itself, which just occurred to him in 1968 and suggested in embryo a film-idea about the mind. Letting his mind 'wander', the drawings were begun, then animated and shot. These were followed by several hundred others. 'The animation was done by inbetweening the whole drawing with the next one, which at times had no relationship . . . I then rolled the film back, did more drawings and shot them. I also included some live-action shots in the third run. These were staged then shot on the fourth run. I wrote a letter in prose form to President Nixon asking him to please stop the war, or else—this more fully to hold the whole thing together.' The film was then left in negative in the can until the Spring of 1971, 'for sentimental reasons only'.

WALERIAN BOROWCZYK

Le Phonographe
(France, 1969)

Using an old phonograph of 1905, with wax cylinders, the film presents a competition between two original cylinders of the period—'The Charge of the French Army' and 'The Mio', a violin solo. Both sound and image are suddenly cut, as if the film had broken in the projector. The technique used is object animation combined with still photography; which results in a form of poetic documentary. The music as recorded on the wax cylinder recalls nineteenth-century sentiment as well as the heroics of the time.

JOHN HALAS and HAROLD WHITAKER

To Our Children's Children's Children
(Great Britain, 1970)

This film is based on the music of an intellectual group of pop artists, The Moody Blues; it attempts to find a close relationship between the music and the visuals. Back-projected lighting and multi-image, split-screen visual composition are some of the techniques used. The back lighting provides a simple means with which to create abstract visual shapes of such pure colour that they resemble stained glass windows.

STUART COOPER
ARTHUR K. BUTTEN

The Test of Violence
(Great Britain, 1969)

This film was based on paintings by the Spanish artist Juan Gerrovés, and is a study of violence in contemporary society. Gerrovés uses fragmented images, to express a form of movement analysis which is a natural extension of the film medium.

GEORGE DUNNING (supervising director)
(directors)
ROBERT BALSER
JACK STOKES

The Yellow Submarine
(Great Britain, 1968)

The film is based on a collection of songs by the Beatles; it introduces several novel techniques and contemporary graphics in a feature-length production which is basically pop-art in style.

© King Features Syndicate—Suba Films Ltd. 1968

NORMAN McLAREN

Pas de Deux
(Canada, 1968)

Norman McLaren applies a scientific approach to his film-making, which helps him evolve new technical formulae in many cf his films. In his latest, *Pas de Deux*, he introduces the technique of **multiple image.**

Norman McLaren writes:

'It might be of interest to readers to have a description of the technique of my latest film *Pas de Deux* (*Duo* in the USA). Although this is strictly speaking not an animated film, it does incorporate some features of animation, in the sense that the final images were synthesized—and of course, animated films are entirely synthesized.

In the original shooting of *Pas de Deux*, no attempt was made to get a multiple image. The dancers, dressed in white, were filmed against a completely black background and black floor. The shooting speed was mainly at 48 frames per second, to give a slight slow-motion effect.

The multiplication of the image was done at a later stage in an optical printer. In the projector of the optical printer we used high contrast positive (Kodak stock 5362) made from the original negative; in the camera of the optical printer we used stock 5234.

To create the multiple image, we exposed this high contrast many times successively on to our new optical negative. The same shot was exposed on itself, but each time delayed or staggered by a few frames. Thus, when the dancers were completely at rest, these successive out-of-step exposures would all be on top of each other, creating the effect of a single image: but when the dancers started to move, each exposure would start moving a little later than the preceding one, thus creating the effect of multiplicity.

The average number of exposures was eleven. The amount of stagger varied from shot to shot, and also within a single shot. A 2-frame stagger created a tightly packed chain of images; a 20-frame stagger made a very widely spaced chain; an average 5-frame stagger gave images that overlapped, but were distinct enough to be separately identified.

Two methods were used to collapse the image-chain into a single image. In the first, as mentioned above, we would have the dancers come to a natural stop and pause. In the second, at a suitable moment in the action, we would optically freeze a frame of the first exposure long enough to let all the other exposures in turn catch up to and freeze on the same frame. When the last exposure had caught up, we would have a single, unified static image, which, by having all the exposures proceed again, this time in step with each other (that is, non-staggered), would continue the action as a single unified image.

If we wished this single image to spread out once again into many images, we would have to optically freeze all exposures except one, allowing only this one to proceed, then allow each of the other exposures in their turn to proceed, with, say a 5-frame delay between each.

In addition to having black backgrounds, it was essential to have back lighting on the dancers. Normal front lighting would have led to visual clutter when the images became multiplied. Delineation of the dancers by as thin a line of light as possible gave maximum readability when the multiplied figures were in motion.'

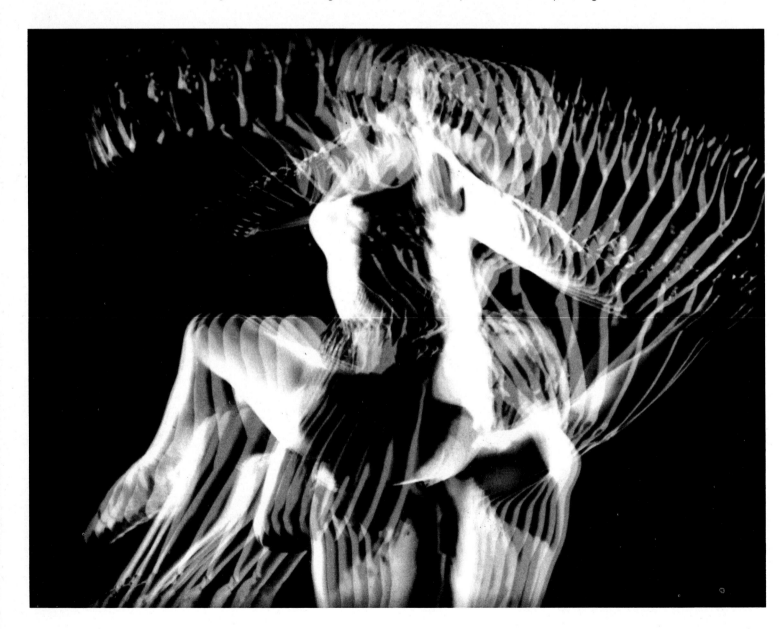

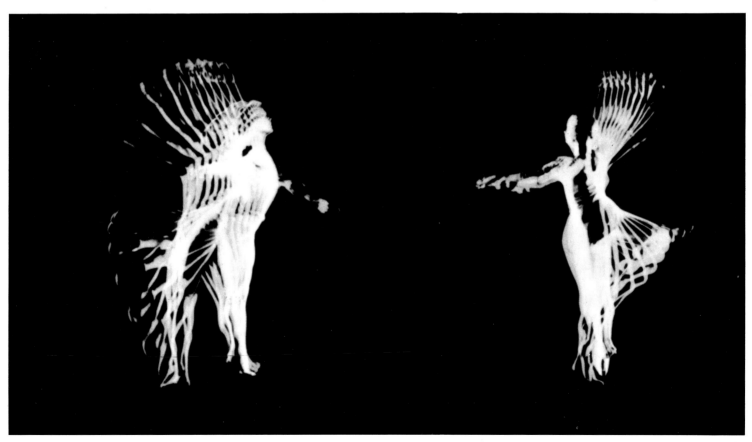

LEN LYE

Len Lye re-established himself as a pioneer during the early 1960s, adding a new dimension to his earlier work in the 1930s.

His early work was confined to painting directly on to celluloid film and animating the sequence in close synchronization with music, but recently he has combined kinetic art with the art of motion pictures. This later work is an excursion into electronic mobile sculptures which he calls 'tangible motion'. He believes that 'motion is a sensory thing of the body, not an intellectual thing of the brain. So first dig the sensory self deep before conceiving either

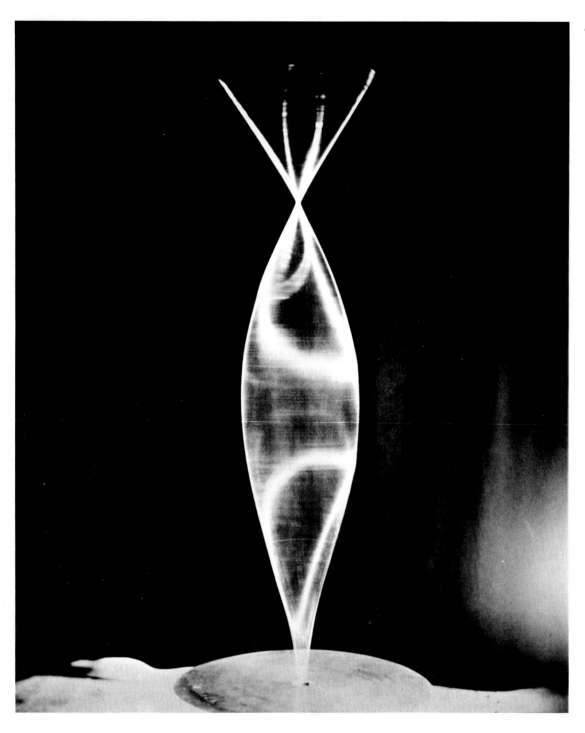

Rotational Harmonic
(USA, 1961)

literary personification or kinetic theory by which to guide the shape of the motion image.'

Of the relationship between kinetic art and film, he writes:

'Kinetic art is the first new art since prehistory. Although the realistic and abstract image both appeared in prehistoric cave paintings, it took till this century to discover the art that moves.

Had we taken the qualities of sound as much for granted as we have taken those of motion, we would not have music. Now, in kinetic art, we have begun to *compose* motion. We project our bodily

Black
(USA, 1961)

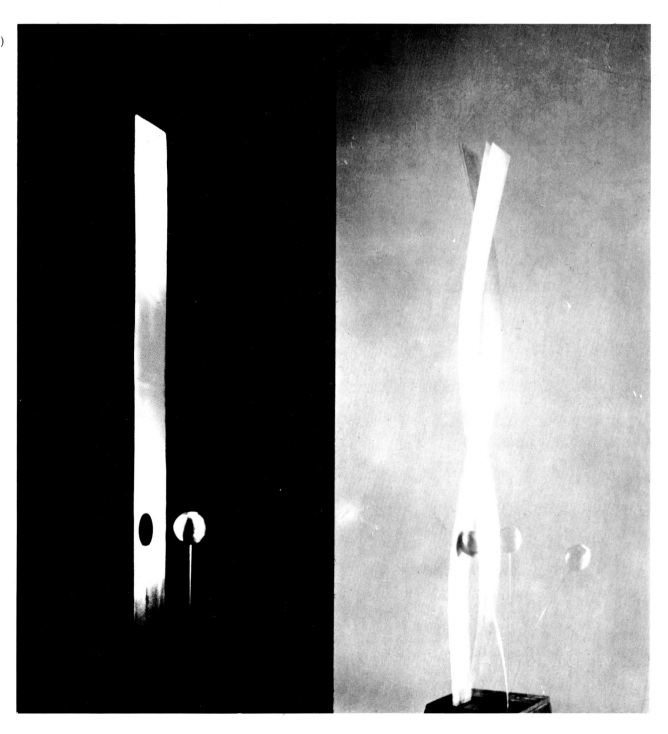

sense of motion beyond the aesthetics of the dance by composing three-dimensional motion sculpture and by editing the sequential composition of motion in film.

The sense of motion is anchored to our unconscious sense of bodily weight. Walking, standing, sitting, running, eating, reading, sleeping, are all performed with a continual holding-balancing-manoeuvering of our bodily weight, which is the organic source of our psychological sense of freedom. Our inherent skill in the timing and control of motion is vital to our existence.

Only static art can hold the emotional mark of its creator in one instantaneously perceived image, one that may invoke an immediate aesthetic response. On the other hand, of all art forms, the imagery of motion best describes itself. It's why we say the sparkler 'describes' the figure 8: we mean the object defines its own action.

Scientists seem to refer to the individuation of energy when they speak of the 'directional' force of evolution. I believe that this force is the same energy which drives the creative imagination; but my point is that *I don't think that the creative imagination is a purely brain-generated, brain-held thing.* I believe that the creative imagination results from the evolutionary force of individuality being sieved through the whole matrix of our temperamental cast, which cast includes the gene pattern and bodily senses both carried by the body.

For instance, I was once experimenting with some abstract jiggling shapes in a film I was making: vibrating dots and dashes which whirled, pulsed, squiggled and darted out on the screen in a repetitive way, particles of energy in space. After fifteen seconds the repetitive action on the silent screen was monotonous. So I found some music to fit the movement: African drums. On its own the drum was monotonous. Drum music was conceived for dance, stimulation coming from the vital progression of the sound rhythm. As the music required literal bodily action to enable one to retain its sensory appeal, so did my film require a counterpart fulfilled by the music. Watching the film images jiggling and darting to music took the place of dancing, and gave an experience of aesthetic emotion on a sensory level.

Energy is the essential element in the enactment of our life span, which is organically and psychologically organized to refine, symbolize and further the essence of our individuality.

I believe art is going to be the final religion, because only art retains the emotional truth of individuality.'

Steel Fountain
(USA, 1963)

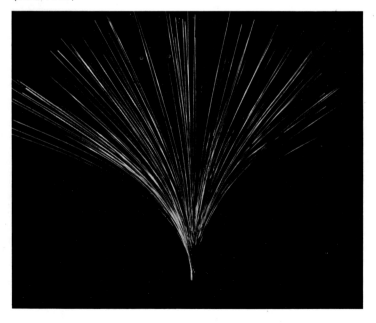

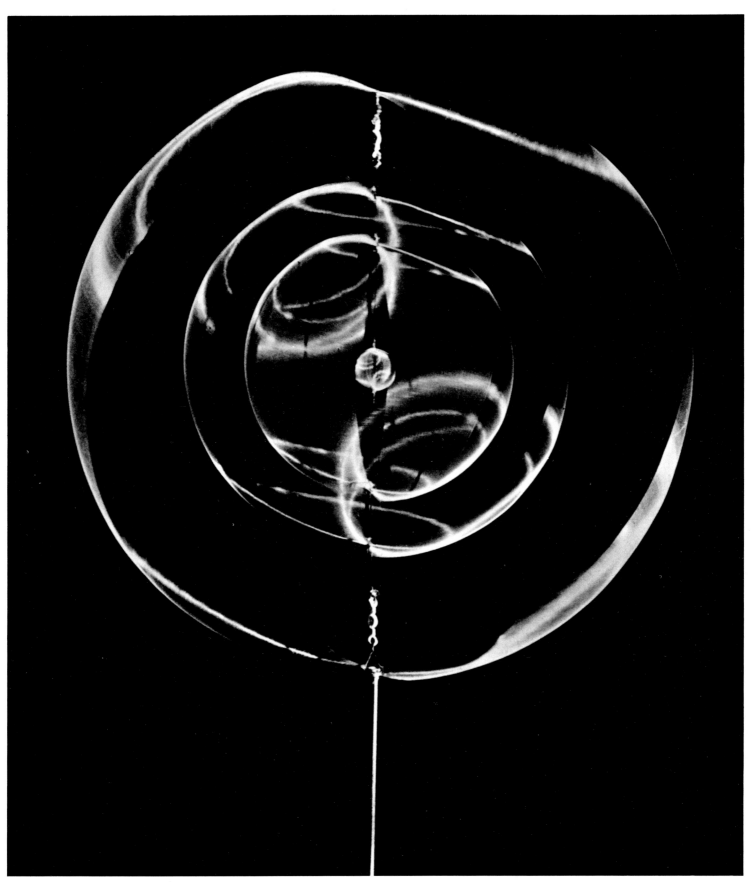

Roundhead
(USA, 1964)

SUZANNE OLIVIER

Waooh
(Canada, 1969)

In this film Suzanne Olivier makes use of *moiré* patterns. Animating these patterns under the rostrum camera, she is able to achieve incidental abstract effects, without animating frame by frame.

MAURICE BLACKBURN

L'Ecran Epinglé (Cine Crime)
(Canada, 1969)

Maurice Blackburn uses the pin-table technique established by Alexandre Alexeieff during the mid-1930s. The method consists of displacing a number of pins and photographing each position frame by frame to achieve a smooth tonal composition through the resulting shadowing. This provides a surprisingly beautiful textural image though the operation is very time-consuming.

TOUCH PINS ONLY WITH RECOMMENDED MATERIALS
ALWAYS APPLY PRESSURE AT RIGHT ANGLES
NOT PRESS ON MORE THAN ½ SQUARE INCH AT

STANLEY KUBRICK

2001—A Space Odyssey
(Great Britain, 1968)

This film combines live action, stop-motion object animation and stop-motion cartoon animation, as well as a comparatively new method of *front* projection of background. Consequently, it was an extremely complex film to make because the technical aspect of the film dominated its total conception. The production story-boards, design and planning had to be exceedingly elaborate in order to resolve the many technical difficulties. The film is an example of how scenes of highly special complex effects can lead to results of striking visual quality.

Many new problems had to be solved, one of them being the passing light that was shed by the rushing meteorites during the final journey in space. Douglas Trumbull, who was in charge of this technical phase in the film, describes the method he used to achieve this effect:

'Employing a technique of image scanning as used in scientific and industrial photography, this device could produce two seemingly infinite planes of exposure while holding depth-of-field from a distance of fifteen feet to one and a half inches from the lens of an aperture of *f*/1.8, with exposures of approximately one minute per frame using a standard 65-mm Mitchell camera.

After the stargate, there follows a series of fantastically delicate apparently astronomical cataclysms. The images implied exploding stars, vast galaxies, and immense clouds of interstellar dust and gas. Without revealing too much detail, I will merely say that these effects involved the interactions of certain chemicals within a camera field no larger than a pack of cigarettes.'

Douglas Trumbull worked closely with Stanley Kubrick, and designed jointly with him most of the special effects in the film, including the split-scan device here described.

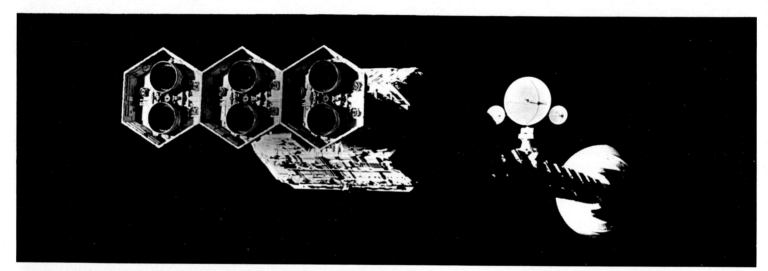

BERNARD LONGPRE

Tête en Fleur
(Canada, 1969)

This film experiments with line drawings in the style of etching.

DUŠAN VUKOTIĆ

A Stain on his Conscience

(Yugoslavia, 1969)
Dušan Vukotić writes:

'Animation offers a possibility to unite the past, the present and the future in one single moment. I have in mind the all-time-round-dimensions of a cartoon. Neither a physical law nor an idea inhibits animation: not even our usual conception of space, time or substance. And just this aspect of a total possibility which animation offers, results usually in fear, initial uncertainty, and in not knowing how and where to go. When I create a scene, I sometimes make hundreds of drawings and then destroy them again—not because I feel that the next one would be better or perhaps worse, but because I know that it could still be different in its structure and its movements, and therefore in its life.

Jiri Trnka used to speak about the resistance of materials, the material of which a puppet is built for example, or of which her dresses are made. Then I had to think that an animator has to be concerned with the *idea* of the material, not the material itself. Apparently these are essential differences. I was never interested in films using puppets or in the animation of objects—I preferred to struggle with a drawing and with its poetical and ideal potentiality, to struggle with its methods of conception, that is, with the metaphysical aspect of an idea and not with the physical resistance of a real object.

It is well known that "timing" is the first and the most significant characteristic of animation; modern animation reduces the time factor to the minimum.

Each animator must solve this problem individually. The mechanical filling-in of in-between phases between two extremes is about to be given up. Each phase represents creative work for me. There is some similarity between an animator and a conductor in that phases resemble notes; you may know the importance of each, but they can still be combined in many ways.

All these are highly practical things; there is no need to make a mystery out of the animator's profession. Ideas and conceptions are most important: what is to be expressed and why animation alone has been selected, regardless of whether we animate a drawing, an object or with a master key a current line on a computer's screen.'

The Yugoslav critic, Ranko Munitić comments as follows:

'A bizarre combination of live-action film and animated picture showing a man who vainly tries to escape from his monstrous tormentor, a slimy spot which persecutes him in a variety of shapes in the streets of the town where he lives. *A Stain on his Conscience* is not adapted from the world of Kafka. The intimate persecutor materializes in the shape of an impersonal but living, active organism which besieges its victim like a strange being from some science fiction story. And this man remains weak, confused and helpless despite his aggressive retaliation to the attacks. He is weak, because morbidity is an inseparable part of his personality, because it has been born out of his hidden complexes.'

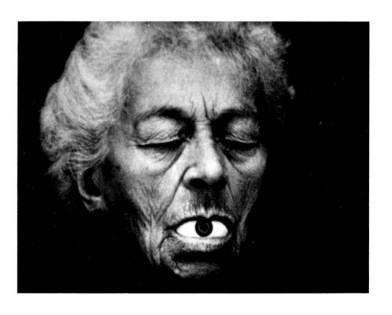

Witold Giersz has become one of the foremost experimentalists in cine-graphics. After experimenting with hand-painted surfaces and integrating these with superimposed animated figures in the film *Little Western*, he developed the technique even further, making an organic unity from these two elements in three more recent films, *The Intellectual (Intelekualista)*, *Horse (Kon)* and *Admiral*.

His technique has all the freshness and immediacy of oil paint actually flowing on to the canvas. The paint is used as a plastic, mobile element out of which animated figures emerge. The pictorial composition is good, but the choreography and animation are even more imaginative and technically creative and skilful.

Giersz's work points ahead to new possibilities and techniques in animated painting.

The Intellectual
(Poland, 1969)

Admiral
(Poland, 1969)

Horse
(Poland, 1968)

YOJI KURI

Miss Kemeko
(Japan, 1969)

Kuri is the leading experimentalist in Japanese
animation, combining a surrealistic style of
pop art with the Japanese tradition; his
type of humour appeals to Western audiences rather more than to the Japanese.
Most of his films do not exceed two minutes,
but within this short space he manages to
convey his own particular kind of concentrated comment.

YOJI KURI

Concert in X Minor (Elegy)
(Japan, 1969)

JOSEF SVOBODA
JOHN HALAS

The Anger of Achilles
(Great Britain, 1968)

A plan for a stage production, based on a story by Robert Graves and produced by Sam Wanamaker, which incorporates the use of film. The technique combines maximum mobility of stage action with film projection, using 42 separate screens. The experiment applies kinetic principles to the stage.

PETER FOLDES

Je, Tu, Elles
(France, 1969)

This new feature length film in colour by Peter Foldes was produced in co-operation with the Research Service of French TV and Films de la Pleyade (Pierre Bromberger). Peter Foldes writes:

'This is a mixture of straightforward live action (my own script), collages and animation. This is a new formula I really believe in. The story is told in the normal manner, filmed roughly like any other modern film, but is able to go further—into dreams, aspirations, fears, past reality, even to sensuous, mystical or metaphysical experiences.

This may sound a little pompous—but fortunately the film is a comedy.'

ROBERT VERRALL
JOE KOENIG

Cosmic Zoom
(Canada, 1969)

Adapted from a children's book by Kees Boeke, a Dutch teacher, the purpose of *Cosmic Zoom* is to show man not only in relation to the environment of his planet, and in the grand perspective of the universe as a whole, but also in terms of the smallest known particles of matter.

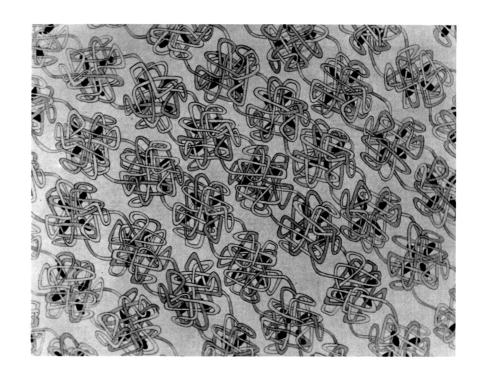

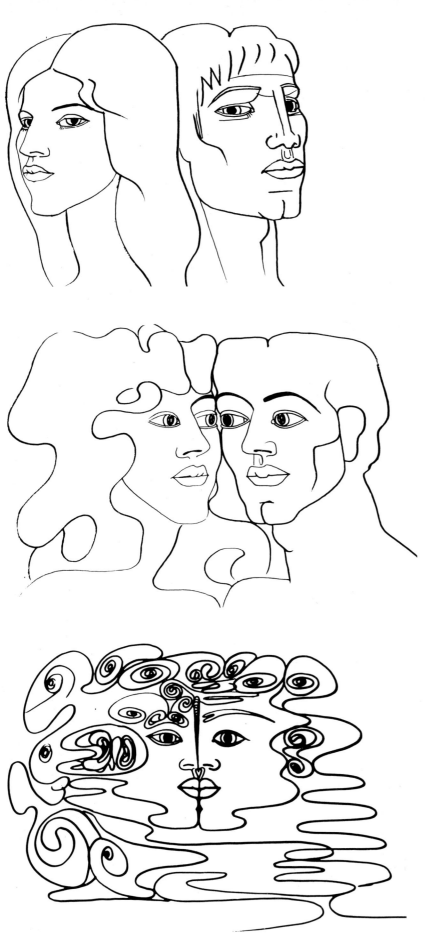

PETER FOLDES

Visages de Femmes
(France, 1969)

Peter Foldes is a painter who can translate
his work into the dimension of movement.
His theme in this film is sensuality.

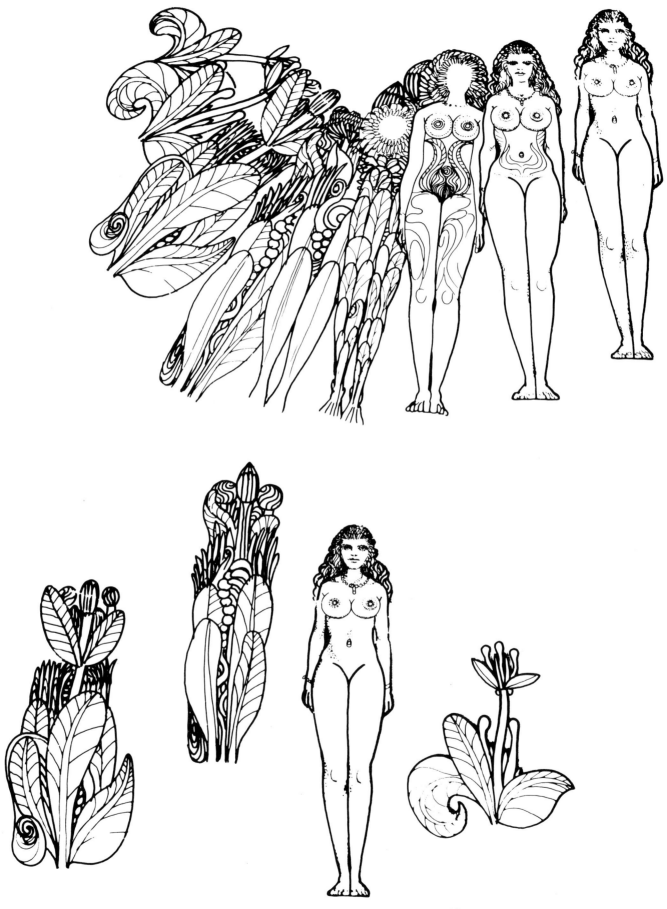

RYAN LARKIN

Walking
(Canada, 1969)

The essential character of people of many different races is reflected in *Walking*, by contrasting the manner in which they move, and the pleasure the act of movement gives them. The film is brilliantly choreographed so that the variant rhythms of walking combine to make a subtle and beautiful continuity of movement between the figures. The film makes use of a variety of technical approaches to animation—classical, rotoscopic, texturized graphics and pure line animation.

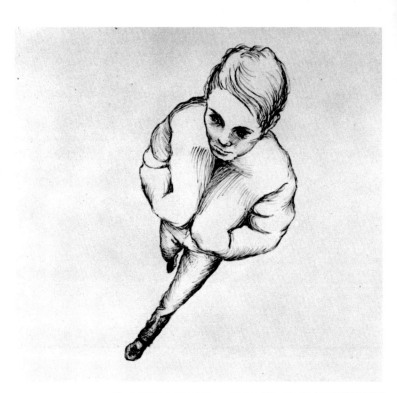

PIOTRE KAMLER

L'Araignéléphant
(France, 1968)

Piotre Kamler writes:
'Why take pains to animate a flower if the wind does it without any trouble at all? Perhaps in order to allow the flower to act in a way it would not otherwise do; become a bird, recite a poem of Apollinaire, or simply disappear. Or resemble no other flower in existence, while still remaining a flower animated by the wind.

Thus there are two approaches which give a *raison d'être* to this generally despised art, and raise it to the noble level of poetry; to make familiar objects perform unexpected actions or to create extraordinary worlds peopled with weird beings.

These two approaches, one literary and intellectual, the other plastic and empirical, sometimes complement each other. Such cases are rare; usually the point of departure determines the result, and one can only illustrate a scenario which has already been decided, or else, starting from a plastic form, seek to understand it and invent its world and its history.

An easy path, which, its direction chosen, leads straight to its target, is limited perhaps, but sure; but a winding labyrinth from which there probably will be a way out, may lead to either a luminous landscape or an irrational abyss.

Which of these two methods is the one to choose? Is the choice possible? Are we not damned in advance by our intellectual origin and our artistic formation? Is not a painter-animator necessarily nearer the empirical attitude which makes him construct the film like a picture, working, by adding

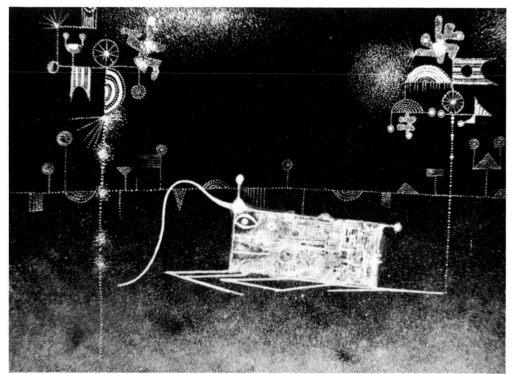

or stripping off a number of successive layers, towards a whole—foreshadowed but not predetermined.

A line, a cube, a six-legged animal, a cloud of dots, an infinite possibility of characters.

What colour, what substance, what movement suits them best? In what décor do they feel happiest? What are their reactions? Is their disposition threatening, humorous or melancholy?

The answer to these questions is a reality which only exists on the screen, solely by virtue of the fact of being seen. Before getting to know it one has to make it exist, put oneself at its service to help it develop.

Slowly, by stages, one sequence gives birth to the next, one character manifests the need to meet another, the need to scratch his back, to walk into a box, to change colour. One is no longer the author; one simply executes actions dictated by an independent situation.

Sometimes the situation grates; forms refuse to collaborate; the movement is wrong. One has to drop it, nothing can be done. The ambition to create is now only impotence before a dead object. But sometimes the result turns out to be enthralling; one discovers an original existence, never seen but perfectly logical. In this case the boundary of the impossible recedes and probability becomes reality. But if one makes up one's mind to manufacture this foreshadowed or dreamed reality out of all the pieces, the reality is at least unique.'

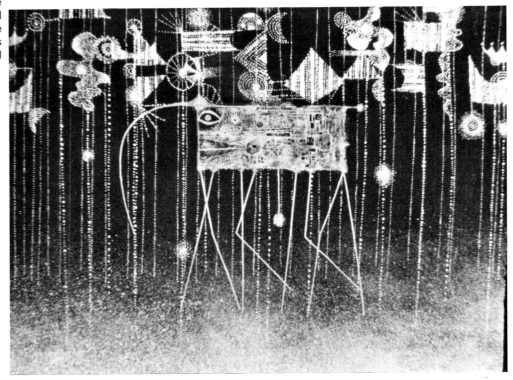

SANDOR REISENBUCHLER

The Kidnapping of the Sun and the Moon
(Hungary, 1969)

This highly stylized picture uses naive motifs derived from folk culture, developed to a high level of sophistication; a parallel can be drawn between this technique and the way Bartok used Hungarian folk music.

EINO RUUTSALO

ABC 123
(Finland, 1967)

Eino Ruutsalo writes:

'I started to make kinetic pictures some time in 1959. I was not satisfied with a mere theoretical knowledge of the film, I wanted to get into immediate contact with it. That is how I began with film emulsion. At one time I had no serviceable camera of my own, so the best thing I could do was to make films without one. I got to know the depths of the picture frame, I observed it in terms of horizontal and vertical movements, I regarded it as lights, colours and reactions. I was able to examine the compositions and calculate the rhythms a frame at a time. I could apply all my experience as a painter to enhance the colour effect of a frame by treating it not in the copying machine but by hand. I treated unexposed, overexposed and underexposed negatives and various positives. I painted transparent surfaces, and scratched black ones. I treated them with colours and exposed them together. I applied beeswax to film and typed on it. I got this etched on film in the same way as titles are etched on foreign movies. I also placed black and white films in various chemicals to obtain surfaces of various values. I made colour film on a black-white budget. I copied additional colour on to black-white-colour film by means of filters of various colours. After getting to know the characteristics of the material in this way, I started to take pictures that I could use as a basis and then "mutilated" them with my own hands by drawing new functions, new events and new depths and planes on the picture film. It is purely a question of the graphic vividness of the picture frame, although I was able concurrently to study rhythmic relationships that were later to prove significant.'

CHARLES JENKINS

Cambridge Steam Engine
(Great Britain, 1968)

This film was specially made to open the 1968 Cambridge Animation Film Festival. The influence of pop art can be seen in the highly individual style of the artist.

JIMMY MURAKAMI
FRED WOOLF

Both these artists have adopted the method of drawing direct on to the celluloid with brush and pencil, and texturize their characters in such a way as to retain their integral visual effect.

This technique represents a contemporary approach to animation which combines the skill of the painter with that of the cartoonist himself.

Along Came a Spider
(Fred Woolf: USA, 1969)

47

JIMMY MURAKAMI
FRED WOOLF

The Box
(USA, 1967)

Good Friends
(Jimmy Murakami: USA, 1969)

Good Friends is one of the first films
sponsored by the American Film Institute
Grant, which is concerned to foster contemporary film art in the USA by young
American directors.

2 New techniques in animation and visual effects

Although both film and television depend for their excellence on creativity and first class techniques, they belong to opposite camps: film to the world of optics, television to the world of electronics. Since cinema is the older medium, it was logical that television should at first derive from it. However, for a long time it has pursued its own course as a part of the electronics industry. In its rapid development in visual communication, television uses an increasingly vast amount of film material, old and newly produced, and so in this respect it has a strong interest in film production. Both have entered upon a stage of advanced specialization in practically all their branches. Many sciences are involved at one stage or another in the production process—chemistry in film stock manufacture and laboratory processing, physics in optics and in sound and colour reproduction, mathematics in camera equipment, in the design of film projectors and computer animation, not to mention the psychology of perception for measuring and ascertaining the effect of the film on the audience.

It is impossible to be an expert in all the sciences which affect the making of a film. Nevertheless, it is necessary to have some general knowledge of the potentialities of the many techniques available in modern film and television production. Graphic designers who come into film-making for the first time rarely understand this. Creative skills, for instance, are closely linked with what can be processed in film laboratories and what sort of film stock is used for a particular visual effect.

Film stock [1]

Knowledge of the characteristics of the film stock is normally the responsibility of the cameraman. Today the five leading film stock manufacturers—Kodak,

[1] Further reading might helpfully include the following books:
Making and Coating Photographic Emulsions by V. C. Zelikman and S. M. Levi (London) 1964.
Photographic Emulsion Chemistry by G. F. Duffin (London) 1966.
Photographic Chemistry by P. Glafkides (London) 1958.

Ilford, Ferrania, Gavaert and Agfa—provide a very wide range of negative and positive stocks for different purposes and for widely different light conditions, as well as for cameras designed to use films ranging from 8 to 65 mms.

The base of the actual film itself is acetate, which is composed of short cotton fibres left by the textile industry. Modern film stock is emulsion-coated with several layers of light-sensitive cellulose acetate. In between the different emulsions, there are other layers of chemicals to act as colour filters and processing barriers. The majority of photographic emulsions consist of light-sensitive silver halides suspended in gelatine. In addition to gelatine the raw material contains silver nitrate, potassium bromide and iodine.

The selection of the right stock depends on the condition and circumstances of photography. Consideration must be given to light conditions, which are measured in terms of foot candles. When filming out of doors, light readings may vary from 10,000 foot candles in bright sunshine to 300 foot candles in cloudy weather. Such variations do not occur in the photography of animation where the lighting and the camera are usually fixed in a static position. The average lighting for animation is 500 foot candles.

The speed of film stock chosen must match different conditions—low speed for strong illumination, high speed for low illumination. For animation the most useful stock is the high speed Eastman colour negative No. 5254 (35-mm) and Ektachrome No. 7255 (16-mm) Choosing the correct lens aperture, which may range from between $f/2$ to $f/5.6$, should result in fine, sharp and clear pictures, both in black and white and in colour. It is relevant to note that approximately 95 per cent of animation is photographed in colour today and a high proportion of it in 16-mm film. For this reason it is worthwhile to realize that the majority of 16-mm photography is carried out on reversal camera film, and only a small proportion uses the conventional negative-positive method, now confined to 35-mm photography. The 16-mm reversal camera stock is either printed on reversal duplicating film, or on to an internegative from which positive prints may be manufactured.

An interesting graphic effect may start with a total disregard for the recommended light reading, exposures, or even focusing. Manufacturers wisely recommend the most useful methods and practices needed to achieve a professional technical standard, but creativity usually starts from that very point.

The physical reaction of any film stock naturally varies with the degree of light treatment it receives, but the level of sensitivity also varies greatly, as between a normal, high contrast black and white stock, and, for instance, the Eastman colour negative film, type 5254. The degree of exposure and the print density affect the final result just as much as the level of illumination.

Films made for use in colour television require even greater attention as far as the type of stocks is concerned. The illumination needs a different approach, since the developed film goes through a series of electronic channels. In spite of the monitor controls, colour and tone distortion is a constant problem.

Film stocks are not especially designed to meet the needs of either art directors or animators. The manufacturers, who have undertaken considerable research into this problem, are concerned first of all to serve their largest market, that of the live-action cameramen, and for them they provide an excellent service. But from the graphic artist's point of view modern film stock is wasteful. In order to simplify laboratory work a negative is used containing all the chemical ingredients of the primary colours, which can then be transferred by a single stage to a final positive. The stock, embodying the full range of colour tones, thus promotes the aesthetic pitfall of realism, which suits live-action production far better than creative animation.

The previous method of colour film reproduction depended on three different separation negatives, each containing primary colours. This gave the film designer greater flexibility and a wider colour palette; but any system which requires too many chemical baths or laboratory light gradings is unsatisfactory and in practice can lead to constant disappointment and frustration when one compares the original concept with the final film. For this reason designers are seeking to find new ways of achieving what they desire to see on the screen. They are trying to bypass the hazards set up by the type of film-making which depends on mass production and systems tailored to the intermediary stages of mechanical reproduction. Photography using high contrast black and white stock, and printing colours from separate black and white negatives is one form of retaining the clarity of colours: the colours are added directly with clear transparent dyes, offering good prospects of clear colour reproduction.

A creative film designer may contribute many ideas after the photography has actually taken place; he can guide or control the manner in which the negative is processed during the key stages in the developing and printing of the film. Decisions as to what effects can be achieved should start in the choice and preparation of the negative and the processes through which it must move; sometimes it must be deliberately over-exposed or an object must be over-lit for a given effect. Such an effect may involve a loss of detail within the shape of a figure so that the figure appears as a colour silhouette, or a loss of detail in the background so that it can be flooded with a pre-chosen colour. In both examples these are effects one could not achieve with normal live-action photography. In a commercial film laboratory working under pressure there is no time for diversions and few of the potential optical possibilities of film are being exploited, yet this is the place where the final effects of the film are produced through processing as part of the creative production line; it may be compared to a kitchen where the meal is actually cooked. The ideal situation would be for the film-maker himself to be able to process almost all existing film stocks, and experiment with timings, the temperature of developers, and the various chemical solutions at the processor's disposal. Control of this kind exists in the case of creative still photography; the work here shows a far greater range of graphic experiment than is the case with cinematography. This only goes to show the interesting possibilities which still lie ahead in film production. Eventually, however, most studios must control their own experimental processing facilities as an integral part of production. This could be quite practical in the case of experimental and sponsored film production, since, compared with live feature production, the length of such films is short, and this in turn means that in most cases processing could be dealt with by hand.

In live-action production, the control of the light reaching the negative film is a major creative and technical concern. Usually it is the responsibility of the lighting cameraman, who leaves the physical handling of the camera to others. His role has been compared to that of a painter, mainly because he is responsible for the visual content and atmosphere of a scene. He has a wide range of tools for achieving his effects—different lenses, a multiplicity of specialized lamps from beam spots to heavy flood lights, as well as defusers and filters designed to achieve atmospheric and colour effects. In graphic films all these effects are conceived by the creator through the laborious preparation of drawings or paintings on celluloid and backgrounds. The exploitation of light effects in a more direct manner using mobile colour lights as a source of animation with the actual film material has still to be developed. It has already shown its enormous potential in mobile graphics.

One simple example of the above is the exposure of a colour film in the dark against the oncoming traffic light in a busy street. The light source exposed appears to be printed on to the film as a moving abstract pattern. Using the same principle on the rostrum animation table, a wide range of colour mobiles can be created. Most rostrum camera tables are fixed with a back projection panel where the light source can be housed and activated. The panel can be fitted with opaque glass for colour definition. With comparatively little labour the colour lights can be manipulated frame by frame and exposed on the same negative stock several times to achieve an abstract colour effect of soft luminosity, and motion similar to kinetic light mobiles. A further advantage of this technique is that primary colours can be retained in a purer form than would be the case if these effects were conceived by painted celluloids or backgrounds photographed by conventional methods. The variety of abstract tones and forms can undergo infinite change compared with direct drawing techniques.

Stop-motion camera

Unlike the live-action camera which is driven by the motor at a speed of 24 frames per second, the animation camera can be stopped by a special device in between every frame, hence the term stop-motion animation camera. Insufficient use is made of this camera's capacity for creating an illusion of movement with a static image. The camera can create a wide variety of movement and, if properly planned, it can be used as a creative as well as a reproducing instrument.

In both cinema and television the powerful effects achieved by fitting zoom lenses on to live-action cameras, allowing a scene to be photographed from a distance or close up without cutting, were a great innovation. A zoom lens attached to either a 16- or 35-mm camera can provide a focal length over a range of 3:1 to 10:1, or even 20:1. Animation cameras, however, have been provided with automatic focusing devices as a standard fitment for a long time. It is possible to move to and from an object with great ease and achieve the same magnification of field sizes as are possible with a live-action camera. Although an animation camera can only move in one dimension, towards or away from an object, the table on which the object is fixed is capable of travelling in all directions from south to north, from east to west, and also rotates 360 degrees. With these movements and with the camera's ability to be advanced film frame by film frame, a high degree of motion flexibility is possible with a single static drawing. It is also possible to analyse minute details of a drawing or painting from the field size of 32 inches down to the dimension of a postage stamp. If the production of the film does not require the use of celluloid changes the whole operation can be automated. The latest computerized rostrum cameras are also capable of carrying out an automated celluloid change which not only makes the operation quick, but avoids the possibility of human error.

With certain formulas of rotational motions and dissolves, and with the employment of automatic zoom devices, the animation camera has become a highly creative tool in the hands of the film-maker, as can be illustrated by the film *Cosmic Zoom* (1969) by Robert Verrall and Joe Koenig (Canada). With the exception of the beginning and the end, which use live-action, this ten-minute film consists of a number of static drawings to which the camera brings movement. It zooms away from a boy in a boat on the river to show his surroundings and eventually the world; from the world, it views the universe, and then goes beyond the universe in a continuous act of motion. After a pause, the camera performs the reverse action, tracking into the boy's hand to a point where a mosquito has inserted its proboscis; the camera continues its journey into one cell of blood, into a molecule, and eventually into the smallest micro-organism known to man. In this case the camera itself becomes the principal actor.

Camera mobility specially favours films in which it is essential to emphasize and maintain the full range of tones and textures of the visuals. Some of Bruegel's and Bosch's paintings with their delightful details were especially successfully revealed by the animation camera in *The Axe and the Lamp* (Bruegel) and *Paradise Lost* (Bosch). With careful choreography and selection of camera field sizes the camera movement is able to compensate for an apparent lack of actual animation.

Special effects

The physical mobility of the stop-motion camera, if used properly, can provide added dimension to a static design. It is also able to analyse forms and shapes in detail. However, its greatest advance lies in the variety of manipulations which can be undertaken with the lenses, and with the camera itself, which in turn enables fluid movement and a wide range of visual effects to be achieved. Apart from the automatic follow-focus mechanism and automatic zooms, which were introduced some time ago and are fitted to the rostrum, a further range of cinematographic manipulations exist.

These newer technical facilities include:

COMBINED MEDIA (LIVE ACTION/ANIMATION)
BACKLIGHTING
SPLIT-SCREEN
MULTI-SCREEN
MULTI-IMAGE
SKIP FRAMING
FREEZE FRAME
REVERSE ACTION
SPINNING ROTATION
RIPPLE DISSOLVE
COMPUTER-MADE FILMS

Operations such as fades, dissolves, superimpositions, panning and tracking are not referred to here. These can be achieved with any standard modern rostrum camera, though in the very latest equipment they have become automated, and can be controlled by a single electronic compound.

Combined media (live action/animation)
Certain facilities are available for animation and graphic effects, which are not dependent on photographic technique alone, and it is regrettable that the cameras incorporating these facilities are seldom used to their full potential.

Perhaps the best example is the stop-motion camera devised by John Oxberry in the USA for the exploitation of special effects, such as split-frame photography, travelling matte, high contrast photography and pixillation techniques, together with special attachments for aerial image photography, and for automatic dissolves and fades. The use of these facilities saves time and money, since many of them were, until recently, carried out in laboratories as a separate process. Most advanced cameras, however, are fitted with automatic adjustable dissolves capable of mixes from eight to twenty-eight frames; other services provided are automatic focusing and an automatic cycle device to facilitate the changes of cell cycles—a cycle being the repeated use of a sequence of cells, giving the illusion of continuous movement. This device allows for the continuing photography of cycles, ranging from three to twenty-four cells, or from two to twelve, provided the photography is double frame. One of the main advantages of an automatic cycle device of this kind is that it minimizes the damage to cells, and saves considerable time if the cells are to be handled frame by frame. Another important facility, which is inadequately exploited, is the use of still photography; zoom photography of a still, for example, can be controlled so that strobing effects are reduced to a minimum, while the accuracy of both timing and direction of movement is complete. A tri-motion effects device fitted to the rostrum camera provides an automatic movement north, south, east or west, while a rotational facility can give to a static drawing the impression of live-action photography.

The aerial image unit is a highly ingenious device, used to match foreground animation with live action. It is fitted with a self-contained projection unit underneath, a process projector which is interlocked electronically with the camera. The unit combines live-action photography with animation in one continuous operation, dispensing with the need for making travelling mattes, which is a time-consuming process and not always accurate. It projects the live-action film through a selection of lenses, like F/e. 5 Micro-Nikkor or Cook Speed Pancro (50-mm) $f/2$ lens, by means of a reflecting mirror set under the table top. The animation, coinciding with the live action, is added, and the two are exposed normally on to a single negative. The projector has a fixed-pin registration film movement which is of the same type as that fitted to the camera. The whole unit is provided with four 400-foot spools, two to feed in and two to take up—a bipack operation. The action is automatic and synchronized, running forwards or in reverse as necessary. In spite of this interlock between the live-action and animation controls, it is still possible to use the peg bars for diagonal movements, although the table is incapable of tracking movement. Nor is there any restriction on the use of the various other devices with which the camera is fitted—wipes, the split-image prism and lighting effects.

The advantages afforded by these technical devices have already been proved by the increased requests for animators to provide optical effects, especially in television commercials. At least half of all television commercials involve some form of effects manipulation, and the demand for the older kinds of animated line-drawing techniques has diminished.

The aerial image unit is primarily used in television advertising where live-action photography is frequently merged with visual effects which can only be provided by animation. For example, the product can only be emphasized by changing shots, mobile letters, or transitions of graphic animation over live characters.

Backlighting

If an opaque plate glass is placed in the centre of the camera table, the table can be used for backlighting purposes with light fittings underneath. This floor unit is fitted with five photoflood lamps and a cooling blower. Such a unit provides facilities for photographing and testing animated line drawings, as well as a variety of interesting colour effects. With this source of illumination the transparency colours retain a unique purity which would be impossible to match with normal painted colour pigments. The coloured light reflected from backlit transparencies can produce an effect similar to that of illuminated stain-glass windows. The potentialities of this device remain quite unexploited from the creative point of view.

Split-screen

The conception of split-screen technique goes back very early in cinema—at least to the French avant-garde cinema in the 1920s. The first Cinerama presentations in the early 1950s were, in effect, physically split, since they used three separate 35-mm films which were projected on to a single screen in synchronization and in register. Often, however, the divisions were kept separate deliberately. Three different angles of water-skiing, for instance, were shown split on three separate screens at the same moment. By this means the action was made more spectacular and its dimension increased. Today there is no longer any technical restriction on how a frame can be split up or fragmented, since the original negative is not divided over three separate reels. With a single negative and the use of a bipack system, or back-projected live action and added visual effects, the operation becomes simple. It is also possible to restrict the screen to one section with a black surround. Usually the screen is divided into sections with one part containing live action, and the other animation, with no overlap between the two. Such a technique can combine actuality—a man's head bent deep in thought, for instance—and animation used surrealistically, with the inside of the head shown schematically to represent the man's thoughts. The method is especially effective in wide-screen systems, where the sheer size of the screen gives ample opportunity to combine live and animated techniques at one and the same time.

The aerial image camera provides the most simple method of combining live action and animation on a split screen, providing automatically the live-action section through back projection and the animation by celluloid overlay and photographing both at the same time on a single negative. But if two live-action shots are involved, two or more exposures will be necessary with a matting device to obscure the second exposure. While it is possible to accommodate this operation in the camera, a laboratory optical is safer.

Multi-screen

Several examples of the use of this technique have recently been seen during the various World Fairs at New York, Montreal, and Osaka. The first notable attempt was made by Abel Gance in Paris during 1925, in his film *Napoléon*. Forgotten for thirty years, the concept was revived by Josef Svoboda, the Czechoslovakian stage designer, who, first of all with his Magic Lantern presentations, and later with his Diapolyekran, a mosaic series of 112 screens, developed the system further for Expo '67. Since then several other film-makers have developed variations of the idea.

The basic concept is to manipulate images projected on different screens. The images can be timed either to synchronize with each other or to counterpoint each other visually. It is possible to leave some screens black in order to focus attention on others. Fragmentation of images within the individual screen, or the creation of one single giant image using all the screens, is also possible. Nor need the screens be static: as seen in Diapolyekran screens, they can be moved forward towards the audience, adding physical dimension to the pictures. In some instances the screens can be placed on the ceiling or floor of an auditorium to achieve the desired effect. Provided the length of films is properly worked out, the system provides a welcome break from the conventional academy-sized static screen to which the cinema exhibition has been chained for over half a century. The freer use of screens also brings cinematography much closer to its basic origin in the kinetic arts.

Multi-image

The basis of this idea is to use the screen, no matter how big it is, as a canvas. With the freedom of a visualizer, one can multiply the same image at will, or use only a small part of the canvas. Or one can expand the image, and manipulate the pictures out of sequence or time continuity. This system in some ways complements the multi-screen systems, both in its visual effect and its revolutionary departure from presentation conventions. Unlike the previous system, only one projector and film negative is involved, though one may utilize larger negative formats like the 65-mm negative and the 70-mm positive films, which obviously have greater visual impact. Wide-screen processes, like Cinemascope, Superscope, Panavision, Cinerama, Cinemiracle, Vistavision, and other large format systems are not at all essential to the multi-image technique; excellent examples of the creative uses of the system can be seen in 16-mm format. So far its principal use has been to create dramatic effects. A direct shot projected on to a very large screen is capable of overwhelming audiences by its sheer scale, an effect which many producers have tried to achieve. Feature films have used the technique, showing a multiplicity of facets of the action at once in an entirely non-realistic and often sensational way. This approach is in keeping with the character of our century—in which a multiplicity of actions are being carried on at the same time.

From the technical point of view it is comparatively simple to reduce an image and multiply it to its desired scale by the use of optical printers. Both the Oxberry and Acme printers are capable of reducing an image in one step, to one-fifth of the original 35-mm dimension. This automatically provides for a range of multi-images which could include twenty-five individual pictures within a single frame. Each reduction requires a separate optical operation, but there is no limit to the degree or scale of the reductions; only artistic judgement is involved together with financial considerations.

The normal aerial image camera can carry out the same operation without bringing in the optical printer, provided the individual sections of a scene making up the multiple image are already photographed in the same positions that they finally appear in on the negative; subsequently each section will be matted out (i.e. masked) in the camera in turn.

Skip framing

This is a technique by means of which certain frames are omitted, while others are introduced from the original negative. According to a preconceived plan, one uses either every other frame of a scene, or selects a staggered series of frames for final continuity. The camera can be set automatically to skip a number of frames at any pre-selected point as long as there are not more than twelve. This technique is especially valuable when one combines live action with animation. The effect of omitting frames is to speed up the action. For instance, skipping over five frames and using every sixth, gives the appearance of speeded-up action to the extent of six times. In normal live-action shooting, provided the right motor is fixed, it is comparatively easy to speed up an action by exposing a scene more quickly than usual using, say, 18, 12, or 8 frames a second, or to slow it down by exposing 36, 48 or 64 per second instead of the normal 24 frames. What the regular live-action camera cannot achieve is to skip or stagger some frames. To achieve similar effects a special optical printer would have to be used. Since animation is preplanned from the start, and the camera can be advanced frame by frame, this problem hardly arises. Credit titles in television constantly use this method, though not always to the best advantage from the creative point of view.

Freeze frame

This is the term used for holding a moving picture stationary over a number of exposed frames. The technique has become an accepted convention in all kinds of television films, as well as in documentary and feature films, since it can often contribute an interesting visual point to the story. Since the animation camera is arrested to take a photograph at every single frame, to freeze several stationary in the same position is easy. It is not so easy with a live-action camera with an automatic running mechanism. In order to arrest a single frame and hold it for a duration of time, the negative must go through an optical printing process. From the point of view of timing, for example, a freeze frame held stationary for two seconds allows an audience a satisfactory view of a character in arrested motion. Shorter holds provide a striking effect, while a hold for six frames creates the illusion of jerky movement. Continuous freeze of four to two frames give a stroboscopic illusion of movement. The widest use of this method so far has been in the production of television commercials and titles, where a freeze frame has a logical place in the presentation continuity of a pack.

Reverse action

This method, as its name suggests, involves the reversal of an action, so that it appears to take place backwards, defying gravity and refuting the progression of time. Only film is capable of such magic, and the release from actuality comes as a relief to the imagination as the early period of silent film burlesque discovered. Live-action photography still requires optical printing to achieve such an effect, but with the animation camera it is comparatively easy to obtain it by reversing the direction of the camera motion. Several additional effects can be achieved with the animation camera by running it backwards. If a circle is gradually traced backwards, frame by frame, and then projected normally forwards, it will appear as if animated forward. With superimpositions and proper planning, reverse photography can substantially enrich a scene and save much time for both the director and the cameraman.

Spinning rotation

This purely mechanical motion is used to achieve the kinetic effect of spinning. The electronic compound which controls the motion of the animation stand has converted it into a mobile stage where any directional motion is possible. The animation stand can swing around automatically 360 degrees or any part of it and in addition to this motion within the stand, it is also possible to attach art work on to the rolling pegbars capable of moving north, south, east and west, so providing diagonal movement. Live-action cameras are quite unable to achieve this degree of flexibility, but to get a similar effect it is quite practical to project the live-action shot up to the aerial image plate, and to carry out the action under full control so far as the speed and direction of rotation are concerned. If additional visual effects are needed, these can easily be added to the back-projected live photography without matting out the original scene.

Ripple dissolve

This is used, especially in television commercials, to soften the movement of a hard object, or make objects appear or disappear with a flourish. If certain ripple glasses with distortion capabilities are photographed over the animation at a preplanned speed and correct exposure, the effect can provide the illusion of soft reflected water which would be difficult to achieve with hand animation. The softness and liquidity effect can be further accentuated by photographing the overlaid distortion glass out of focus. Surrealistic effects can also be created through slow dissolves, similar in fact to Len Lye's kinetic mobiles, *Tangible Motion, Sculpture* and *Oscillating Steel Fountain,* which combine the fluidity of water with the force and flexibility of steel in another dimension.

Television technology, with its flexible and precise control over the wide range of video signals, can achieve most of the effects described here, especially ripple dissolves and reverse action. Sometimes such effects can be created better and quicker by passing the video signals through some frequency selective networks—the electronic engineer has great latitude of control over such effects. Nevertheless television, even the 625 lined colour monitor, does not provide adequate definition to make such effects useful for the cinema screen. This observation need not apply to the future, especially since newer cathode ray tubes are available to the computer industry with much higher line definitions. If these could be utilized for special effects work, the two industries could come closer in this field of production.

Computer-made films

Computer-animated film represents only a small part of the wide range of a computer's capacity in the production of graphics. We will only be dealing here with film production.

The great asset of the programmed computer is that it is capable of transferring electronic impulses, at great speed, which can be made visible on a cathode ray tube in the form of moving images, and then photographed on to a negative film; there is no reason why this should not be used by film-makers, educationalists and scientists alike. This same conclusion was reached by many artists and electronic experts in the United States as far back as 1964.

At the beginning of 1965 the Bell Telephone Laboratories in New Jersey, under the guidance of Dr Edward Zajac and Dr Kenneth Knowlton, began experiments which led to the production of a number of what have now become well-known computer-animated films. Among these are K. C. Knowlton's *A Computer Technique for the Production of Animated Movies* (1965), F. W. Sinden's *Force, Mass and Motion* (1966), A. M. Noll's *4-Dimensional Hypercube* and *Computer Generated Ballet* (1966-7), E. E. Zajac's *Two-Gyro Gravity Gradient Altitude Control System* and *A Pair of Paradoxes* (1966) and Stan Vanderbeek and K. C. Knowlton's *Man and his World* (1967). These films, as their titles imply, range from hard scientific instruction in space research to pure experiments in the visual arts.

The production of computer-made films spread fast, and today well over a hundred establishments are involved in this work in the United States alone. These include General Electric, Westinghouse Electric Co., IBM, and most of the space research units, as well as certain prominent universities. Consequently, the number of computer-made films produced during 1968 reached (according to the estimates of the Computer Animation Committee of the USA) approximately 250.

Such sudden expansion of activity is not unusual in the United States. Nor, unfortunately, is it unusual for it not to be paralleled in the United Kingdom. American investment in the development of this new medium exceeded $10, 000,000 by 1969, while in the United Kingdom it was no more than £3000. Apart from the work of a few enthusiasts at University College in London, little was done. The initiative in Britain was finally taken by Halas and Batchelor in 1968, and the following year two experimental units were co-operating with them in the production of a series of computer-made mathematical educational films (one at the Department of Computer Science, University of Edinburgh, with Dr J. V. Oldfield, the other at the National Computer Centre, Manchester, with Dr F. E. Taylor and Maurice Russoff). So far two films have been completed, *Ellipse and Circles* and *Pole and Polar*, but many more are contemplated.

The mechanics of producing an animated film by computer require a special technique, a special language, and a close co-operation between the visualizer and scientist.

Of the many production systems in existence, the most flexible is that developed with the high speed digital computer. The instruction for programming pictures to control this digital computer is based on the Fortran language, which writes formulae in terms of symbols rather than numbers. Fortran is the most frequently used all-purpose computer language, and a special version has been advanced by Bell Telephone Laboratory for film-making during the last few years. The other suitable language is Beflix, developed by K. C. Knowlton, who is also at Bell Laboratories: this provides richer visual tonal variations in its final effect.

Both languages lead to the transference of images directly to the microfilm recorder, which displays the picture in the form of a large array of spots of differing intensity of light. These may be exposed on film. While Fortran transfers drawings in terms of lines and curves, Beflix provides a flashing of areas with specific shades and tones, resembling a painting more than a drawing. Beflix may suit film-makers better. Unlike the Fortran system, which relies on a numerical code to activate the computer, the Beflix system is based more nearly on a pictorial code, and consequently requires little mathematics—an advantage, one might think, for artists.

The operation is simple. To start with, the instruction is fed into the computer. The computer instantly calculates the necessary numbers which will specify the picture as well as the progression of the film. The information is put either on punched card or magnetic tape, and transferred to the microfilm printer. The instruction is then conveyed to a decoding unit, which converts it into analogical waveforms. Amplifiers activate the waveforms, which are positioned and intensified as electron beams on the face of the cathode ray tube. The electron beams form an instant image on the cathode ray tube which can be held there for any time desired. The tube is phosphorized, so the image is extremely bright. A photographic camera is linked to the tube and records the image on film. The microfilm can be compared to a painter's brush, and the cathode ray tube to the canvas.

The whole process happens at a greater speed than is possible with human labour, and provides a greater variety of pictures. The image is created by the microfilm printer in the form of points, lines and a various number of shades. The cathode ray tube is a very sophisticated piece of equipment with an electronic gun, a matrix in front of the gun, and a receiving capability of 1024 by 1024 resolutions. This means that the micro-printer can activate over a million points on the viewing screen of the cathode ray tube—1024 horizontally and 1024 vertically. It is a unique proscenium for an electronic ballet, especially if the variety of possibilities in shading is also taken into account.

The graphical computer most suitable for film production is the SC 4020—an improved version of the SC 4060 manufactured in San Diego, California. One of the initial teething troubles was co-ordinating the pulse rate of the electronic beam on the viewing screen of the tube with the speed of a film focused on it in the camera. Jitter and image-spreading were problems which have now been overcome through better synchronization and the use of double perforation register pins to carry the film smoothly. Both 35-mm and 16-mm cameras are built in as standard equipment in the computer.

The process still involves some difficulties. Film-making, even through a computer, is an exacting operation. The exposure must be just right. The displacement of one stop can upset the delicate balance of the vector intensity on the viewing screen, preventing some vectors from being seen or over-emphasizing others beyond the original intention. Another problem is the laboratories' inexperience in handling the negative. Usually the film must be developed for 'high contrast' processing in a bath intended for positive prints. Unfortunately, such requests have resulted in the past in a completely fogged film. Although the ultimate aim will be to accommodate processing and optical as part of a computer film operation, for the time being laboratories will have to be involved in the operation. The two functions must be co-ordinated more closely, since the wide variability in quality of the original film exposed by the microfilm recorder involves special precautions and a higher degree of care in printing from that of a normally made film.

At present, the leading organizations producing computer films are the Boeing Aircraft Company, the Lawrence Radiation Laboratories, the Bell Telephone Laboratories, and the Polytechnic Institute of Brooklyn, all in the United States. The latter have devoted a considerable amount of time to simplifying the Fortran language for the programming of films, so that the method could be easily available to all who might benefit. PIB's own system is called Polygraphics and this is probably so far the most useful guidance, using a SC 4020 or 4060 computer. Other instructions, slightly different from the above, are available for running programs on the IBM system 360/65 computer through the newly established Computer Animation Committee in the USA.

Some of the many improvements that could be made to computer animation have been described by Professor Ludwig Braun. They include:

1 Subroutine calls, with storage allocations and insertions. This could save time and make excellent use of the computer's capacity as a memory store.
2 Ability to achieve such standard camera techniques as pans, wipes and zooms with simple calls.

3 The ability to define various regions on the screen as windows or shields, that is, regions in which writing is permissible and those in which writing is inhibited, respectively.

4 Straightforward means for labelling, titling, and general text writing, with the ability to justify the text along the left or right margin, or both, or with respect to the top or the bottom of the region.

5 A set of 'SAVE' routines, which permits the programmer to avoid re-computing parts of a frame which remain constant over a significant number of frames by saving the SC 4020 code corresponding to those frame elements to be repeated. This can save a great amount of computer time.

6 A set of vector routines to permit vector operations, such as dot- and cross-products, which would permit considerable programming simplification in many cases.

7 A set of projection routines for producing orthographic, perspective and stereoscopic projections of objects defined in the computer.

8 A set of routines for setting up to run a movie (e.g. to produce automatically a 200-frame blank leader and a 200-frame blank trailer).

9 Scaling of the screen, and of the several regions defined by the user, separately, and at his option.

10 The ability to manipulate regions. A previously-defined region may have its scale changed in respect to the screen scale; it may be moved or rotated in respect to the screen axes. All picture elements defined in respect to the region axes and contained within the region move or rotate with the region.

To this day, few of these problems have been solved.

There are many obvious advantages in developing computer-made films. Scientific research is one of them. Films for education is another outlet. Artistic and technical experiment adds yet another inducement. The sheer speed of production is, perhaps, the most significant advantage of all.

E. E. Zajac's films of the motion of a communication satellite, such as *Two-Gyro Gravity-Gradient Altitude Control System,* could not have been realized by orthodox methods. The changing perspective, with the complicated differential equations which were required to stipulate the involved rotations of the satellite caused by the effect of gravity, could only have been achieved through a computer. Since this film, the method has been used by all satellite researchers as an integral part of their experiments.

Mathematical calculations and constructions are tried out by computer animation. The Nobel prize-winner, Dr G. Von Beskey, devised a mathematical model of the basilar membrane. A film was made with this model to find out how the membrane behaves under certain conditions. Sound waves entering the ear travel from the base of the membrane to its summit, causing the membrane to vibrate in a different manner. Its slowed-down action is clearly shown in the computer film, and as there are several thousand vibrations per second, one is able to study for the first time how and what happens to the physical aspect of the spoken word in the inner membrane of the ear.

Another field explored has been that of aerodynamics. The Boeing Aircraft Company completed a film of their aircraft's landing behaviour before the craft was built. They also made a film on the vibration extremes of the aircraft. The Lawrence Radiation Laboratory in California made some films about the earth's weather conditions and about the propulsions of a shock wave in a solid object.

The Engineering Department of Syracuse University has made a number of films concerning the composition of complicated period wave forms by adding extra projections on to an axis of rotating vectors. The effect is a three-dimensional presentation of a scientific phenomenon which would not have been possible by any two-dimensional means of demonstration.

Another method is medical research. The action of the interior of the heart has been reconstructed on film by another American university and, for the first time, both the doctor and the patient can see in three dimensions the characteristic motion of the heart. Computer animation is an ideal medium for medicine, science and engineering.

The creative potential of the computer is an aspect of the visual arts of growing significance. This whole field is full of new possibilities, but it is difficult, probably undesirable, to draw a sharp line between functionalism and creativity. A film made by Robert Reynolds and his colleagues at the Los Alamos Scientific Laboratory, showing the action of fluid wave motions in contact with a hard wall, was of exceptional beauty, almost like a Leonardo da Vinci etching in motion. The limitless possibilities are, however, beginning to excite an increasing number of artists, stimulating both fantasy and imagination. IBM in New York have already given a three-year grant to the artist, John Whitney, to enable him to experiment as he likes, while Stan Vanderbeek, the experimental painter, has worked with the Bell Telephone Co. in New Jersey. Computer Art Societies have been formed on both sides of the Atlantic, and a rapid expansion of interesting experiments can be anticipated in the near future.

However, the cost of computer animation has to be considered. Costs are not easy to calculate since it is difficult to account adequately for the research and capital investment in computer construction which lies behind every film made by its means. Nevertheless, the Brooklyn Polytechnic Institute has established a charge of $200 per hour of computer use, which appears reasonable. Other institutes charge on the basis of each frame in the film on a scale of 10 cents a frame. These costs, of course, leave out all the other items of expense, such as preparing the script, the storyboard, programming time, tapes and optical and processing charges. Leaving these aside, the cost of computer animation could be fairly evaluated at approximately half the current rate for orthodox animation production. However, the element of speed with which one can produce a film compared with hand-drawn animation may in the end prove even more valuable than these advantages of cost. Once the preparation has been completed, the production run for a short film only takes a few minutes. The laboratories, however, add considerably to this time before a showprint is available. Introducing the computer into the production of animated films has had an irreversible effect. The performance of the Stromberg Datagraphics 4020 Plotter has injected the inevitable mark of the Electronic Age into animation which had been searching for a new formula for decades. The computer's greatest asset is that it can perform long, arduous and repetitive calculations at a very high speed.

Experiments and achievements by Stan Vanderbeek, Ken Knowlton, Edward Zajac and John Whitney have proved to be inspiring. There is no turning back— unlike, for example, such other, less significant innovations as the use of *musique concrète*, which led animators into a cul-de-sac of 'trick' scores which are of little creative help. Computer-made films have great practical application, as well as exciting artistic possibilites.

At present the process of computerized animation can only be carried out in the form of mobile graphic images; computerized live-action, for example, cannot yet be contemplated. Consequently, this technique of production needs the participation of animators, designers and layout artists. The game is being played with new tools. The graphite pencil becomes electronic, the storyboard turns into a sensitive cathode ray tube, capable of generating thousands of electronic signals per second. The new language must be learned, just like acquiring the necessary skill to fly an aircraft, drive a combustion engine or tap the keys of a typewriter. The rewards are a widening of vocabulary in visual language and experience, to be welcomed by artists and scientists alike. Nothing as important has happened in animation since the development of cell animation itself.

The new generation of artists, especially those with some mathematical knowledge, should appreciate computer-made films now from a connoisseur's point of view. In the future, however, they will become as acceptable to artists as any conventionally produced work of art. Computer-made art may very well replace the conventional piano at home since it will be possible to combine 'instant' vision with computerized music, and enjoy it within the family circle. Although some of the effects outlined may appear complex operations, most of them can be carried out as a matter of routine. Needless to say, their value depends on the creative use to which they are put.

While the animation camera is capable of achieving a variety of effects, there remain some areas where laboratory optical printing is still preferable. For instance, certain forms of travelling-matte process printing, which combines live actors with backgrounds photographed at a different time and location, can be improved. Some aspects of the multiplication of images, texture and diffusion effects, fog and fragmentation images can also be achieved more effectively in this way. There is, however, a strong case for having the visualizer in control of these operations instead of the laboratory technician.

Contemporary audiences are able to observe details on cinema and television screens far more readily than their predecessors. They can take in, or 'read', far more than is usually offered to them. The eyes become an observing instrument of the greatest complexity through experiencing the density of our modern society. Constant visual stimulation of the right kind is essential in order to keep interest alive. For this reason alone, the creative artist must take advantage of every effect offered by the new range of visual facilities.

JIRI TRNKA

Ruka (The Hand)
(Czechoslovakia, 1966)

Ruka, which deals with the subject of the creative freedom of the individual, is a brilliantly conceived film using the three-dimensional medium of puppetry. Several sections of the film break away from the plastic, three-dimensional treatment with abstract colour continuities, but Trnka never loses full control of the various complex forms he employs.

J. A. SISTIAGA

Scope Color Muda 75
(Spain, 1970)

Sistiaga's paintings are here expanded into the dimension of movement, the abstract images being painted directly on the film. This is his first feature film and a pioneering work in the category of painted films.

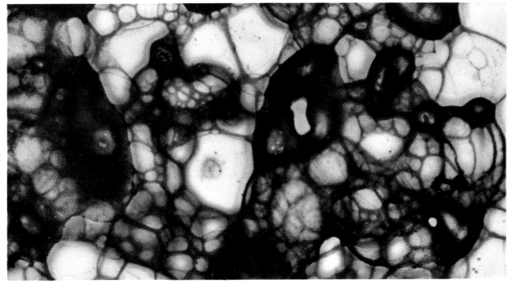

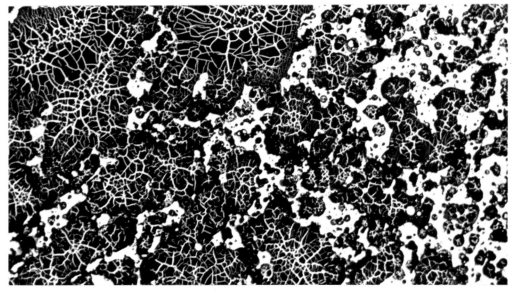

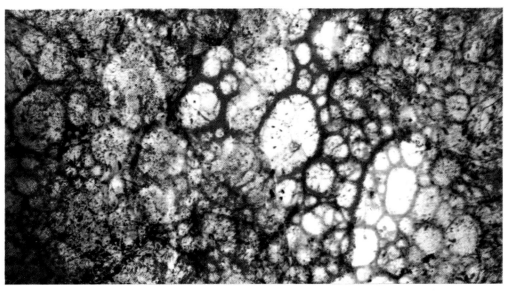

JAN LENICA

Adam II
(Germany, 1969)
(see page 72)

JIRI BRDECKA
FRANTISEK BRAUN

Hunting in the Woods
(Czechoslovakia, 1967)

The style of the romantic painter, le Douanier Rousseau, is successfully adapted here for animation.

JAN LENICA

Adam II
(Germany, 1969)

Adam II is Jan Lenica's first feature film; it was made in Germany, took three years to create, and needed 150,000 stop-frame exposures for 80 minutes running-time. It is a surrealist image, described as a 'sad contour-face which reflects all its experience in a poetic universe', a universe in which the infant interacts with the computer which is programmed to control him. The film projects an electronic hell which embodies and projects the philosophies and pressures of our self-destroying age. Every process from eating and speaking to hearing and thinking evolves like a room full of automatic games, together with every kind of manipulated sound—an incessant shrilling, shaving, sawing, hurling, humming, growling, knocking, shrieking, squeaking, sucking, booming, clucking, grating, crunching. This 'adventure in graphic art' has been described as 'ideas and happenings' which are 'logically and inevitably inspired by the technical aspects of the cartoonist's art'; in its jumps from phase to phase it 'combines Chaplin's clowning with the Golem's threat', while the characters are animated with cuckoo-clock life. Lenica's landscapes seem to consist of gigantic finger-prints or details blown up from old etchings. The film was made in collaboration with Boris von Borresholm, with music by Anton Riedi.

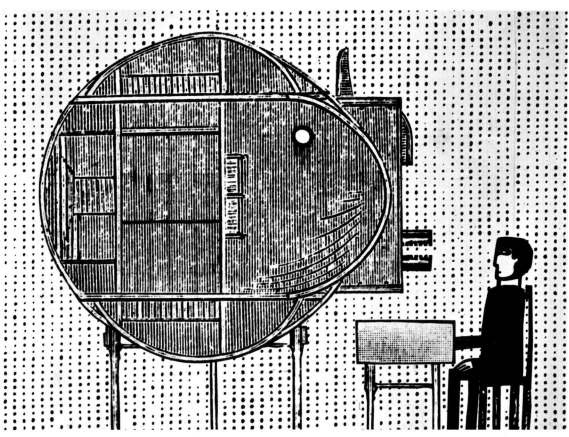

JOSEF KLUGE
HANA STEPANOVA

The Gossips
(Czechoslovakia, 1969)

Surrealism emerges in Kluge's and Hana Stepanova's approach to
their stories and graphic style, which employs straight animation
combined with *collage* techniques.

74

RICHARD WILLIAMS

The Charge of the Light Brigade
(Great Britain, 1968)

This series of animated drawings was used as continuity inserts.
Stylistically, they are based on political cartoons of the period,
notably from *The London Illustrated News.*

ERNEST ANSORGE

Fantasmatic
(Switzerland, 1969)

This artist has a very strong tonal sense in black-and-white, together with an equally strong dramatic mood, which is sometimes almost overpowering. The films appear like engravings in motion, especially in the case of *Fantasmatic*, which has striking contrasts in dimension.

Les Corbeaux
(Switzerland, 1967)

SAUL BASS

Man Creates
(USA, 1968)

In this film Saul Bass successfully combines a number of different techniques including live-action, animation, stop-motion, *collage*, and many optical effects.

The theme is the process of creation, and the film is, technically, very significant, demonstrating how the multiplicity of new optical devices can be imaginatively used.

    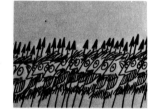

RYSZARD CZEKALA

Ptak (Bird)
(Poland, 1969)

Czekala writes:

'The film *Ptak* was made by the cut-out method directly under the camera, the cutting of the elements and the drawing taking place during animation. In this way I succeeded in transferring the creative process from the stage of conceptual preparation of the film to the moment when it is actually realized.

Since I realize my films myself—starting with the scenario and finishing with the music—and only call on the help of a single assistant (Zbigniew Szymański), they have the nature of a personal statement and their form deviates to some extent from traditional animated cinema.'

There is a close analogy with sound in the construction of this film. The visuals were created to emphasize a sharp contrast between white and black; the same principle governs the sound, where silence corresponds to pure white in the picture. 'At the

same time the structure of the whole film is based on normal rules of visual-aural counterpoint, according to which the sound coincides with action in the picture only in exceptional moments, although in principle it is an element which contributes to the construction. Thus it is almost impossible to decipher the film if it is watched without the accompaniment of effects from the loudspeaker, and the music by itself without the picture seems to be merely disorganized sound. Only the unity of picture and sound gives an artistically complete whole.

For me, methods of realization are of secondary importance, and are usually dictated by the nature of the thought. However, I try to use the simplest means possible, paying most attention to the artistic side of realization (composition, movement, editing). I entirely avoid any sort of technical 'tricks' or striving after effect, since it is not my intention to astonish the viewer, but to use the language of art to convey to him the problems which concern me.

Another important fact which differentiates me from my famous countrymen—Lenica and Borowczyk—is that while with them movement takes place against a graphic background, with me the graphics themselves are, to some degree, made up of movement. Perhaps I have not yet realized this principle consistently, but then again the body of my artistic achievements is not great, and the realization of these conceptions is only now opening up for me.'

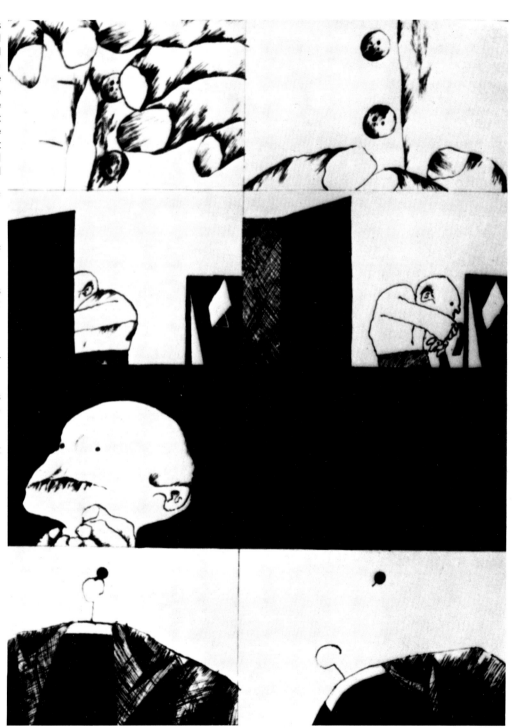

Syn
(Poland, 1969)

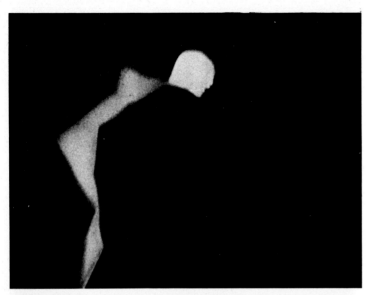

GOLDSHOLL ASSOCIATES

During the last twenty years, Millie and Mort Goldsholl have contributed high quality animated and special effects to television and industrial films. The team incorporates some of the latest trends in their work. Their comments are as follows:

About *Dissent Illusion*: 'Reconstruction of live-action animation into distorted time dimensions by slow camera speed and re-animation.'

Dissent Illusion
(USA, 1969)

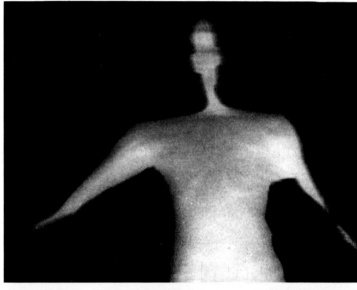

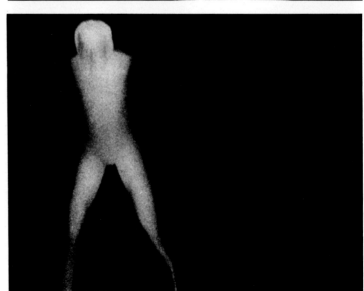

About *Wonder Circus*: 'A wild potpourri of antique and garish forms animated in stop-motion and intercut with wild live-action creates a lively and colourful atmosphere for a proposed television programme on the circus.'

Wonder Circus
(USA, 1969)

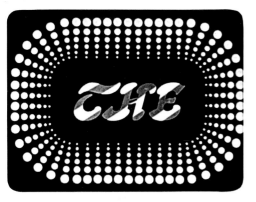  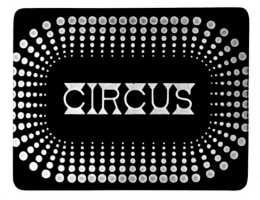

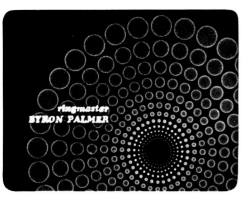  

JOHN and FAITH HUBLEY

Windy Day
(USA, 1968)

Windy Day follows the tradition of closely integrating the texturized
setting and characters. Music, dialogue and movement are perfectly
combined with the animation.

GOLDSHOLL ASSOCIATES

Packaging
(USA, 1969)

The Goldsholls write: 'Set into a live-action film, this sequence is devoted to the graphic excitement that goes into packaging. Colour, design and fast paced animation set to percussive sound'.

Up is Down
(USA, 1969)

'Brings together free magic marker animation sequences showing a little boy who walks on his hands, close-up photography and reconstructed photography animated to highlight his encounters with the fantastic world of nature, and animated news photography projecting some harsh realities.'

EMANUELE LUZZATI and GIULIO GIANINI

L'Italiana in Algeri
(Italy, 1969)

This successful team transfers theatrical design to animated film. Colourful texturization and an ability to relate delicate movement to classical music are qualities typical of their work. This particular film is based on Rossini's music.

JOHN HALAS
HAROLD WHITAKER

Cars of the Future
(Great Britain, 1970)

Children's drawings forecasting future cars were the inspiration for this film. An attempt is made to retain the naiveté, charm and textures of the originals which this spontaneous film reflects. The textured style of animation has been achieved by coloured inks and pencils similar to those the children themselves used.

L. VAN MAELDER

Van Maelder draws directly on the film emulsion and uses strong, bold colours.

The Cage
(Belgium, 1969)

A Visitor

ISAO TAKAHATA

Little Norse Prince Valiant
(Japan, 1969)

The Toie company for which both these animators work has one of the largest animation studios in the world. It produces films, mainly for adolescent audiences, in the style of early Hollywood cartoons. Though the technical polish of these films reflects the skill of the animators, their aesthetic level remains elementary.

KIMIO YABUKI

Fables from Hans Christian Andersen
(Japan, 1968 and 1969)

RAOUL SERVAIS

Goldframe
(Belgium, 1969)

This film presents Jason Goldframe, the great film producer, who aspires to make the first 270-mm film. Servais uses here, as in his previous work *Sirene*, sharp, incisive black and white line drawings to underline the social comment he wants to make.

MANUEL OTERO

Univers
(France, 1969)

Ignorant of the dimensions he moves in, man throws himself against the incomprehensible boundary of his knowledge. To obtain only the barest inkling of the system which encloses him, he must understand that he *is* the boundary, the envelope of all things.

Men live inside spheres—their universe. These worlds are contained within each other. They first mistreat men, then protect them, the infinitely great to the infinitely small.

The film is drawn with white ink on a black background. The drawing changes according to the dramatic development of the film. Bamboo brush is used for the violent and dramatic scenes, a felt-tipped pen, which gives a less defined line, for the emotional scenes, and a wax crayon or a pen for the finely detailed characters.

The most interesting part was giving depth to a design without a background, creating a feeling of volume from simple lines—particularly in two important scenes where the camera travels, making a succession of animated images with a movement of the camera, before settling within the limits of several other animated images, superimposed on them.

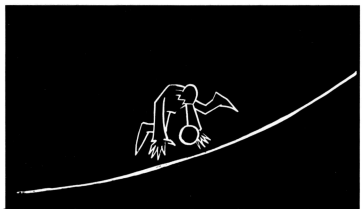

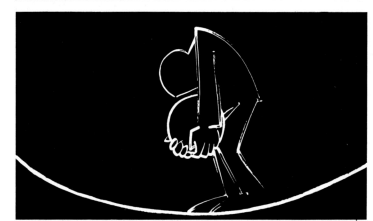

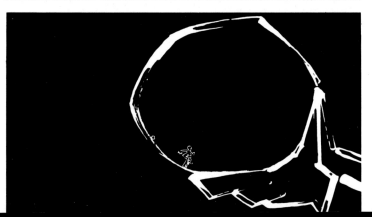

ZLATKO BOUREK

Captain Arbanas Marko
(Yugoslavia, 1968)

This film is surrealist in conception, and shows how the work of the painter can be extended, through animation, into the medium of film. It is of importance in this film that the art of the painter remains dominant throughout.

KAZIMIERZ URBANSKI

Czar Kólek (Magic Circle)
(Poland, 1967)

Animated cut-outs are connected with prepared location shots.

Tren Zbója (The Bandit's Lament)
(Poland, 1968)

Classical animation of a drawing on cels, but by overlapping individual phases on one another during photography 'signs of animation' arise. An invention of Urbanski's called 'lightpainting' is used for the background; he paints with the aid of thermo-chemical reactions.

Fluid Water Flow Dynamics
(USA, 1968)

Computer animation is able to provide certain movements which would be extremely difficult and time consuming to achieve manually, such as accurate movement in extreme perspective and movement in three dimensions.

In certain complex mathematical calculations, for instance, the problem of how fluid water would act if a sluice gate was suddenly raised and the force of water hit a solid dam, can be programmed far more easily by a computer. In this instance, in a film which lasts ten minutes, the computer performed 500 million separate calculations, which would have taken centuries by any other means.

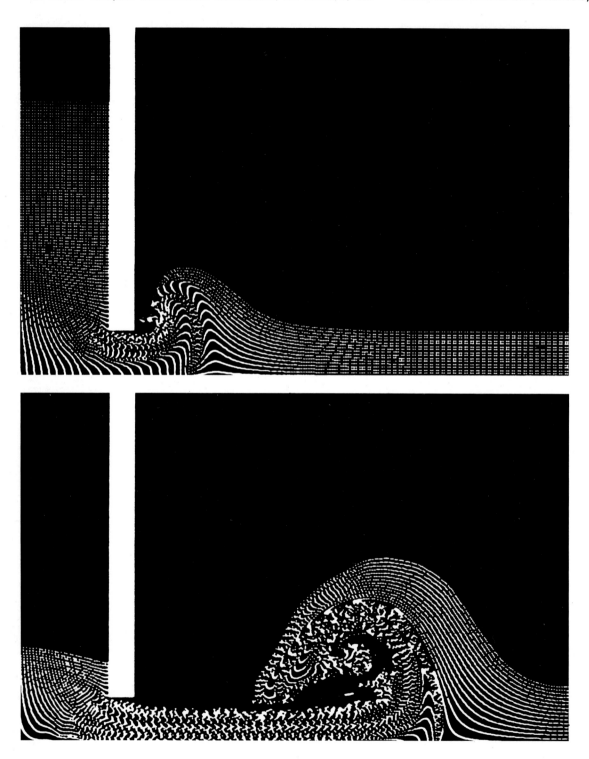

DANIEL SZCZECHURA

Daniel Szczechura is one of the out-standing talents in the Polish cinema. His austere graphic style always illustrates some philosophic point.

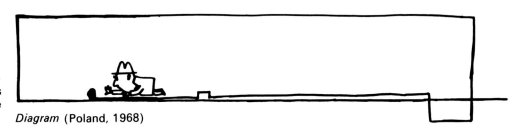

Diagram (Poland, 1968)

Litera
(Poland, 1968)

Karol
(Poland, 1968)

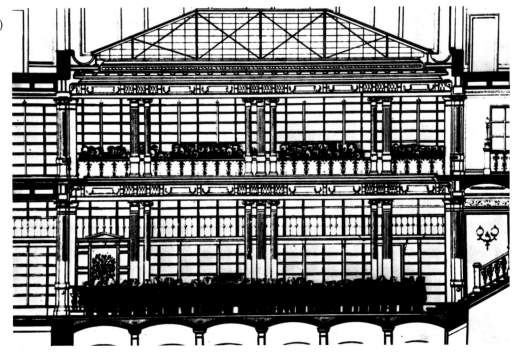

GERALD POTTERTON

Pinter's People
(Canada, 1970)

A one-hour television programme based on Harold Pinter's five short review sketches. These sketches are re-enacted through a mixture of animation and live action, the latter material being photographed in London.

BORIS KOLAR

The Discoverer
(Yugoslavia, 1968)

Ranko Munitić writes that *The Discoverer* presents 'three stories about man's search to discover the limitations of his ingenuity. In the first story a man is making efforts to disperse the darkness around him with the help of a light bulb which must be put in the right place. The trial ends with an explosion and nothingness. In the second story we witness his efforts to light a fire by the most primitive means. And in the third sequence we see the man, who, like a prophet in mythology, calls upon the sun from the peak of a dark mountain by using a horn. But his variety produces first, witches, then satellites, and finally a monster which appears from the darkness and devours the pretentious provocator.'

The symbolism is obvious: the light is a synthesized vision of that unknown but important element which man has to master when progressing through various phases in his life. But is he able to do it? Is he not too limited by the utilitarianism of his values?'

F. KHITRUK
V. ZUIKOV

Film, Film, Film!
(USSR, 1969)

The Russian director, Khitruk, successfully satirizes the atmosphere of a whole studio in the process of a production. The traditional attitude to design of the Russian studios is now giving way to a more contemporary approach. Techniques of animation have always been of a high standard but this skill is now in the process of being applied to more stylized forms.

BERYL STEVENS
(Larkins Studios)

The Curious History of Money
(Great Britain, 1969)

Part of a series of films produced for Barclays Bank Limited. These films have been outstandingly successful, in contrast with similar subjects treated in live action. The style derives from a traditional cartoon treatment involving texturized figures.

Who'll Pay my Mortgage?
(Great Britain, 1969)

(opposite top)
ALVAR ERIKSON
LASSE LINDBERG
ARNE GUSTAFSON

Out of an Old Man's Head
(Sweden, 1969)

This is the first full length film to be made in Sweden which is primarily a work of animation. The animated sections project the fantasies of the old man who is the principal character. Though the influence of the early work of U.P.A. in the United States is obvious, stylistically the film retains something of the national character of Scandinavian art.

JOHN WILSON

Archy and Mehitabel
(USA, 1970)

In this most successful feature-length film, John Wilson applies a contemporary graphic style to a traditional story.

While the freshness of the original story is kept throughout, it is combined with great richness of design and colour.

VALENTINA and
ZINAIDA BRUMBERG

L. AZARK
V. LALAIANTZ

Big Misadventures
(USSR, 1969)

MAX MASSIMINO GARNIER

The Marriage
(Italy, 1968-9)

MAX MASSIMINO GARNIER

Although observing the traditional taste for the grotesque in the Italian cartoon, Garnier brings great originality to his work.

Merendero
(Italy, 1968-9)

3 Contemporary animation: an international picture

For thirty years there has been little incentive for individual animators to experiment with new ideas. The system favoured the factory production associated with the Disney studios. Commercial forms of distribution demanded a regular supply of short cartoons, and the conveyor-belt of production was laid down firmly. Story ideas, gags, model-making, design, animation, tracing, painting and checking departments, sound recording, camera, editing and dubbing departments—at least twenty-four different specialized services were necessary even for a six-minute animated film.

Few productions really justified such a lavish provision of labour. The majority of the films suffered from over-emphasis on 'realism', resulting in smooth, life-like movement and behaviour of characters, and repetition of the same actions and situations. Today few establishments are left which operate this conveyor-belt system. There are some in Japan, and some in Hollywood. The main emphasis today is on work with individuality—individual inspiration in search of new forms in graphic design and the exploration of new techniques, as opposed to using a hard and fast system with sub-divided responsibilities.

This change, reflecting the outlook of almost all leading animators, came as a result of the natural evolution of film-making, as well as the conscious revolt by the film-makers against the misuse of the potentiality of the medium. Today's system of production comes much nearer to producing a Golden Age in animation. In the early period of Pat Sullivan, Winsor McKay and Max Fleischer, story ideas and gags dominated the continuity of the film. Abstract visual ideas which could not be conveyed by live photography were frequent. It was the Iron, even the Bronze Age of animation. Today, the influence of modern graphic design permeates our short films; the characters appear to be highly simplified, but are more expressive because of this, more in tune with the concept of design and stylized humour in the stories, and better integrated with their equally stylized backgrounds. Also, stories penetrate far deeper into the human subconscious than was ever possible before. Some animators are able to investigate on a philosophical level the shortcomings of our society and offer their own sharp, critical comment on what they observe.

These are some of the general values which modern animation has reflected throughout the world. But there are some distinct traditions which are still maintained in certain areas, if not so persistently as before. Commercial pressures in advertising in the West have led to a constant flow of commissions for the animator over the years. The competition for commissions has enforced a high level of technical competence, with the result that films originating in these areas have a smoother continuity, more expertise in timing and action, and more fluid animation. The same qualities are emerging more gradually in certain Central European and Japanese films as well, especially during recent years, but as far as subjects are concerned it would appear that film-makers in Western and Central Europe develop their story content with greater depth and penetration than many on the American continent.

The main regions of production in animation today are:

USA

Animation in the United States is rich with potentiality after a period of stagnation. Exciting new ideas are coming to the surface, both in design and technique, encouraged by the numerous graphics and film students from such film schools as that at the University of Southern California, at Harvard, at the Pratt Institute of Design in New York and at the Institute of Design, Chicago. Out of the five thousand students studying film arts, a number of them have produced films which would easily match professional standards.

Until the late 1950s most animated films, especially those intended for television, were influenced by the skill of the Hanna-Barbera Studio, which is one of the largest in the world. It still continues with the same concept of the animator backed by a gag-writer, but today the emphasis lies on the contribution of the designer and art director, and on the value of visual invention. Animation on its own has become meaningless. Many may regret this development when they consider the dispersal of the highly skilled animation teams which dominated the Hollywood industry for forty years, but the new generation of animators, like Murakami, Woolf and Bob Kurtz among many others, have a far wider range of techniques and design facilities, and are also far more adventurous with the story content of their films. Films of consistently high quality emerge from such artists as John and Faith Hubley, Mort and Millie Goldsholl, Bill Littlejohn, John Wilson, Fritz Freleng and Dave De Patie, Leslie Goldman and Chuck Jones.

Two further areas of production are worth noting. The field of optical effects which was normally left to laboratory technicians, is now controlled by the graphic artist and film creator, who with more efficient equipment can provide optical effects as a part of the service from his own studio. The work of Richard Rauh (Optical Effects Co., New York), for example, shows how mobile graphic design can be combined with live action. Apart from these two extreme techniques he uses other techniques like photo-animation, skip frame animation and animation with three-dimensional objects, and the way he mixes them often provides effects which are novel and visually exciting.

Secondly, the experimental animators have achieved new standards, both through the work of Carmen d'Avino and Fred Mogubgub in New York and the achievements of the newly emerging computer animation in several research establishments and universities. The work of Stan Vanderbeek, Bruce Cornwell and John Whitney has already shown the potentiality of computers as the latest tool in the hands of the creative artist. The possibilities for experimental animation as well as mobile scientific diagrams have been widening gradually due to the initiative of American colleges using the computer.

France

True to tradition, France has attracted a number of artists who have contributed substantially to the art of animation during the last decade—such as Walerian Borowczyk, Jan Lenica and Piotr Kamler from Poland, Arcady from Bulgaria, Peter Foldes and Jean Image from Hungary, Manuelo Otero from Spain, Alexandre Alexeieff from Russia, and Claire Parker from the USA. Paul Grimault, Michael Bouchet, Robert Lapoujade, René Laloux and André Martin have provided the native talent.

Borowczyk's approach especially deserves examination; in such films as *Angel's Wings* for example, he has brought animation nearer to visualizing the subconscious. Surrealism dominates his work, which is always rich and interesting graphically. His choreography and animation stylistically suit his subjects. He has been able to bring the medium nearer to kinetic art than the majority of the animators in Europe. Jan Lenica and Piotr Kamler, who use a three-dimensional form of visual presentation, also adopt a surrealist approach to their subjects. None of these artists is a storyteller—their work is confined to an abstract approach, creating a world of their own. Paul Grimault and Manuelo Otero are interested in telling a story, and they succeed most of the time with fresh and often satirical ideas. Peter Foldes is primarily a painter, but he has used animation as an extra dimension to his work. Alexandre Alexeieff and Claire Parker have a superb technical command of film, and have evolved several novel forms of film-making, such as tone animation with shadows created by the displacement of pinheads. The special characteristic of the French contribution has always been the innovation of novel techniques and revolutionary departures. Unfortunately, in the late 1960s, new ideas did not emerge to the same degree as they did during the early years of the decade. However, with traditional attitudes in France to the arts, and with the present dynamic movement in kinetics and electronics, it is difficult not to think of this country as one of the essential contributors to animated films.

Great Britain

In Great Britain, production in graphic cinema falls into five categories:
    television and cinema commercials
    industrial public relations films
    scientific and industrial training films
    television and cinema titles
    experimental films.
In spite of the fact that the majority of commercials are routine assignments, lively and creative ideas have been used in television and cinema commercials by the Richard Taylor and Larkins Studios, making films for Barclays Bank, as well as in the films of Robert Brownjohn and Trevor Bond for the Midland Bank. These films have inspired in traditional organizations a new attitude towards sponsorship. They are appreciated by the public who accept them as entertainment, which is also good advertising.

Industrial public relations films using animation were initiated in the United Kingdom soon after the war by a series of films made by Halas and Batchelor for British Petroleum and Shell. The tradition seems to have survived into the seventies; it favours contemporary design and is widely sponsored by British industry. It is recognized that drawn film has the ability to make ideas penetrate with a special kind of appeal which holds the audience's attention even when a serious subject is involved. A typical British approach in propaganda films is to base the story on some well-defined argument, and allow the members of the audience to make up their own minds. These industrial public relations films are very sophisticated in content and style, and appeal to a totally adult audience.

Scientific and industrial training films are as much a tradition in Great Britain as documentaries. Technically, they are usually very competent and created by first rate craftsmen. Two developments are worth noting. First of all diagrammatic, two-dimensional visualization has lost its static character. Objects are conceived in three dimensions, especially when the subject deals with chemistry or biology, showing atoms and molecules. Secondly, just as in the publishing world, animated factual films have freed themselves entirely from the traditional visual appearance of the textbook, by introducing a new concept of design into the illustrations. Recent diagrammatic films make use of graphic design more acceptable aesthetically to contemporary students.

Well-designed television and cinema titles can make a valuable contribution to a programme or feature film. However, although the television studios are well equipped with the latest cameras and staffed by talented designers the present range of television titles lacks creative ideas—especially when one considers the opportunities opened up by electronics and the number of different programmes. The cinema has proved more fertile—the contributions of Richard Williams, Robert Brownjohn and Maurice Binders are especially striking and have appeared in many features produced in recent years.

Experimental films occupy an important place in Great Britain, produced not only by units already well-known, like Halas and Batchelor, Robert Godfrey and G. Dunning, but also by the new work of art college students and younger graphic artists. *No Ark* (1969), designed and directed by Abu Abraham, Alan Kitching and Johanna Darke, for instance, is an exceptionally pleasing achievement, with clear graphic design and intelligent timing. Deanna Wisbey's *The Garden* is an exciting exercise both in animation and visual conception. The work of Keith Walker, a former dustman, Wayne Anderson and Colin Mier in the Halas and Batchelor studios promises new ideas in design concept, especially in texturized figure animation. The students of Guildford School of Art, under the direction of Robert Godfrey, are making experimental films far beyond the level of the average student of graphics. In short, British animation is full of promise for the seventies, with great awareness of the potentialities of the medium.

Canada

Animation in Canada owes a great deal to that great pioneer of experimental cinema, Norman McLaren. His approach to film-making has always been based on a balance between technical invention and good design. But his strength is based on his scientific understanding of the film medium, which clearly emerges in many of his films, such as *Mosaic, A Chairy Tale, Horizontal and Vertical,* and *Pas de Deux,* where physical phenomena such as wave motion, perception of vision and motion dynamics are employed.

The high standard of other film-makers at the National Film Board of Canada, like Robert Verrall, Colin Law, Gerald Potterton and Ryan Larkin, can be explained by the fact that they are less subject than most to commercial pressures, and are therefore able to spend a considerable amount of time developing an idea. Time is set aside for the search for new forms and expression, independent of the production of actual films.

Switzerland

The rise of interest in animation in Switzerland should inspire graphic artists to bring the medium up to the high level of other branches of Swiss graphic art and experimental kinetics. So far, however, only E. Ansorge has proved his ability on an international level.

Russia

Russia is a country where good animation has always been appreciated, and where a great tradition exists in the classical style. Ivan Ivanov-Vano has always been able to combine Russian character with international appeal—in his film *The Four Seasons*, for example, which is richly decorative and fluidly animated. Fedor Khitruk, with his latest animation, including *Film, Film, Film!,* has shown a sense of humour equal to that in the most sophisticated films from the West, and the timing of his action is as expert as the best work in Hollywood.

A welcome development towards decentralization has taken place in Russia in the location of studios. New studios have sprung up in the Ukraine at Kiev, in Georgia at Tbilisi, in Estonia at Tallin, and it will be especially interesting to see what new creation will emerge in the recently opened studio at Tashkent in Uzbekistan in the continent of Soviet Asia.

Japan

Japan has adopted commercialized animation at the point where Hollywood left it some years ago. The output is high, but of little aesthetic value, with the exception of the work of a few outstanding film-makers, such as Yoji Kuri. Kuri's abstract design and bleak humour have a special appeal for western audiences, and are in line with the high standard of contemporary Japanese graphic design.

Central Europe

There was an established animation industry in the United States for at least three decades before the last war, as well as a modest tradition in the medium in both Britain and France. The central European countries, however, only showed an interest in animation after the war had ended. The first signs of real excellence were revealed in the puppet films of the Czechoslovakian artist, Jiri Trnka. By the late 1950s, however, some brilliant work was coming from Yugoslavia, which has stimulated experiment in neighbouring countries.

Three outstanding artists have emerged from Zagreb-Film: Dušan Vukotić,

Vatroslav Mimica and Nicolas Kostelac. Vukotić believes that animation, in his view a combination of science, philosophy and poetry, is basically an undiscovered art, and one must be prepared to experiment. In his own words: 'Animation is by its very nature a restless art, and therefore suitable for avant-garde ideas and experiments'. Together with the younger generation of Yugoslav film-makers, such as Nedeljko Dragic, Zlatko Grgic, Zlatko Bourek, and Boris Kolar, the animators of Zagreb-Film have created one of the most exciting centres for progressive film-making in the world.

The Poles entered on a new period of creative activity during the early 1960s with the work of Witold Giersz, Jerzy Kotowski, Władysław Nehrebecki, Lechosław Marszałek, Daniel Szczechura, and many others, who have richly developed the style of Polish animation.

The Hungarians caught up during the mid 1960s, and today artists such as Gyula Macskássy, István Imre, Josef Napp, and Sándor Reisenbuchler are making films of international merit in a fully contemporary style, which yet retain an element of Hungarian folk art.

In Czechoslovakia an impact has been made by the work of the late Jiri Trnka, Karel Zeman, Eduard Hoffman, Bratislav Pojar, Jiri Brdecka and Zdener Miler. Combining craftsmanship of high quality with great technical competence, and good humour with a clear, graphic style, the Czech artists have won recognition throughout the world. The younger generation of Czech artists like Frantisek Vystricii, Pavel Prochazka and Josef Kabrt promises to continue on the same original creative path. One hopes that this established tradition will continue in spite of any difficulties they may have to encounter.

Roumania has Ion Popescu-Gopo and, among the younger generation, Sabin Balasa, George Sibianu and Horia Stefanescu. These artists have less experience than their colleagues elsewhere, but are catching up with them rapidly.

Sweden

In Sweden a new generation of film-makers are creating feature cartoons. *Out of an Old Man's Head*, for instance, by Lasse Lindberg, Tage Danielsson and Per Ahlin will inevitably stimulate a fresh interest in animation in Sweden.

Holland

The Netherlands had three assets: an excellent tradition in fine arts; a first class documentary film industry; and George Pal, who just before the war established a technically superb puppet film unit in Amsterdam, producing films for Philips.

Since then, Joop Ghesing, Toonder and Harold Mack have been active in the field. Lately, however, Ronald Bijlsma and Wim Giesberg are showing promise.

Belgium

In Belgium, apart from the continuous production of feature length cartoons by Belvision-TV, Raoul Servais has made valuable contributions to the art of animation with his latest three films *Chromophobia* (1966), *Sirène* (1968) and *Goldframe* (1969).

Spain

Spanish animation is dominated by the continuous use of television advertising films, few of which are outstanding. However, studios like Moro in Madrid and Marcian in Barcelona, which are also active in other forms, have provided some extremely witty and grotesque films during the mid-1960s. Robert Balser from the United States has been working in Spain, and through his inspiring influence, has managed to upgrade the technical qualities of Spanish animation.

Italy

The value of the Italian contribution lies in their modern decorative design in animation, especially in the work of Emanuele Luzzati and Gianini in Rome, and Max Massimino Garnier in Milan. Pino Zac and Bruno Bozzetto are also artists who have made films notable for their mature humour. The Italian sense of life and gaiety emerges from the work even if the general level of storytelling has not yet reached the highest standards. But some high quality factual animation has been produced by the brothers Elio and Ezio Gagliardo under the name of Corona Films in Rome, and some expert advertising films by the Pagot brothers and Gavioli.

Germany

In spite of the great tradition of German caricature represented by Hans Fischer, Flora and Ernst Gross, this country has not yet been able to support or produce an outstanding artist in animation. Potential sponsorship exists in the television market, together with a strong sense of graphic design and consciousness of new developments in aesthetics; Germany has a public hungry for satire, so without doubt a start will be made in West Germany following the initiation already taken in the East by the DEFA Studios in Dresden where animation has been flourishing since 1955 and the studio currently employs nearly 100 artists.

There are a great number of creative directors producing commercial television films in Denmark, Finland and Portugal. Once these directors become established the next step is to make an experimental film of greater length. These films which often reach international standards are usually produced from the artist's own financial resources.

If one considers that during recent years studios have sprung up in such territories as Mexico, Brazil, Cuba, Morocco, Vietnam, Tunis, Turkey, Egypt, Nigeria, New Zealand and notably Korea, where Young Park's studio now employs over 120 artists, it is difficult to find another art form which spreads more universally than animation. It is a fact that animation is no longer a monopoly of Hollywood, the western and the central European studios. This is a welcome development.

ION POPESCU-GOPO

Kiss me Quick
(Roumania, 1969)

The Director of *Homo Sapiens* continues to use the same broad approach to design.

ADRIAN PETRINGENARU

Little John and the Big Villain
(Roumania, 1969)

The style of the film is based on traditional Roumanian icons.

STEFAN SCHABENBECK

Everything is Number
(Poland, 1969)

Schabenbeck writes:

'The black and white films *Everything is Number, Exclamation Mark,* and *Drought* were made by cut-out technique. *Stairs* was a puppet animation in cinemascope format, also black and white. *Wind* used cut-out techniques and colour.

In *Everything is Number* the cut-out technique proved to be that most appropriate for the type of plastic art I had chosen. However, it turned out that in many places I had to go back to the classical method of development by means of drawings in order to get the smoothness of motion I needed. *Drought* was similar. On the other hand, in my last film, *Wind*, it is difficult to speak of any kind of pure animation technique. Rather, trick shots and cut-outs were combined. This method followed from the problems of filming movement into the depth of the frame with a cut-out method. I used a moving multi-plane set-up combined with a mirror set at a fairly large angle to the plane of the animation table. The action took place on the glass and movement in depth was obtained by animation on dissolves. The active elements were the clouds which move into the depth of the frame. Together with the background of the sky, they are animated on the moving multi-plane in perspective.

Stairs, which is a puppet film, demanded a technical solution for animation in depth which was obtained by using a dolly-crane with

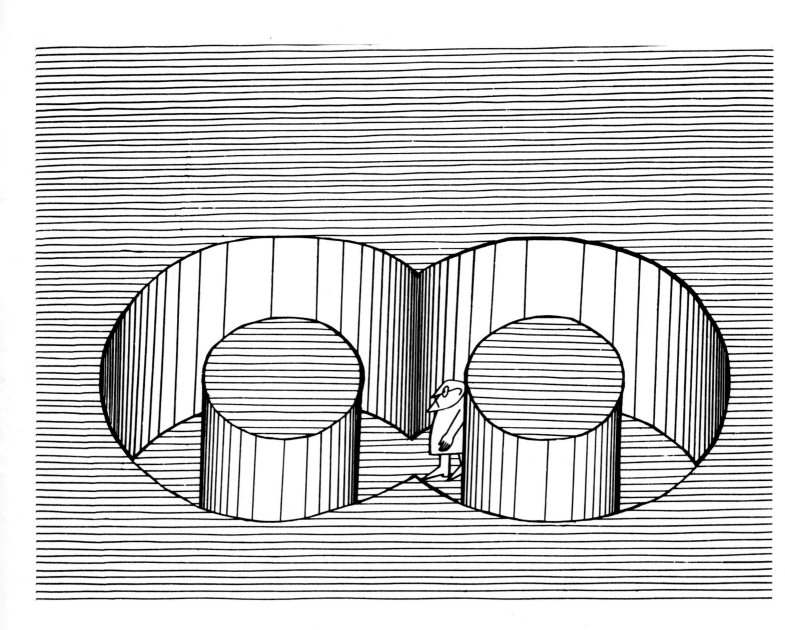

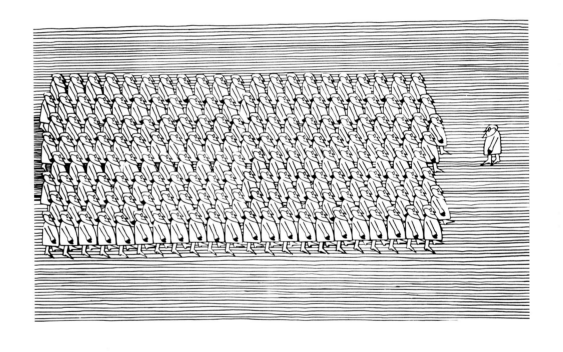

STEFAN SCHABENBECK

three animation screws on which the camera was mounted. The set was three-dimensional with photographic back-drops. Large sets were necessary because of using anamorphic lenses and the need to achieve a suitably large depth of field. The puppet-protagonist was made of foam rubber in order to get a soft, organically 'biological' movement.

Each new film has its own new problems which are often difficult to foresee in their entirety before one starts shooting, and for this reason new methods are often arrived at on the set—plastic solutions which serve the content of the film. The principal aim remains that of solving the problems of content and form.'

Wind
(Poland, 1969)

Drought
(Poland,1969)

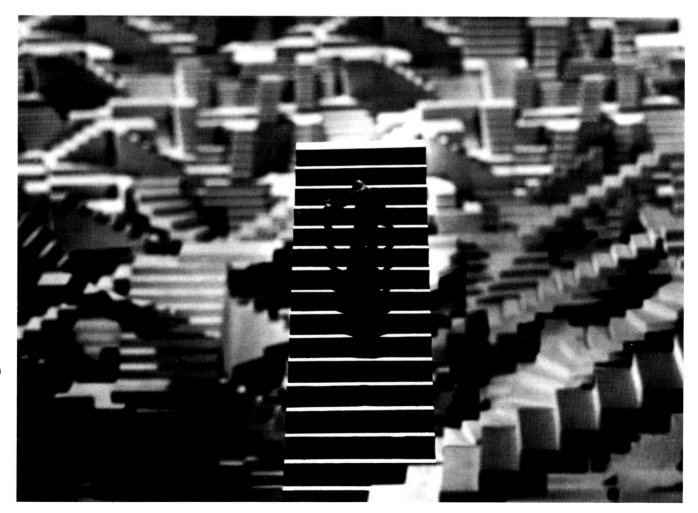

airs
oland, 1969)

STUDIO MORO
Madrid

Directors: José Luis Moro
            Maschler
            Alan Shean
            Robert Balser

Triunfo and *Manos Llenas* are commercials for a weekly magazine.
The first uses paper cut-outs; the second strong line animation carried
out directly on celluloid with photographic collage—the style
inspired by Robert Balser.

Manos Llenas
(Spain, 1969)

Triunfo,
(Spain, 1969)

HILARY HAYTON and
GRAHAM McCULLAM

Egbert Nosh
(Great Britain, 1970)

A series of three, nine minute cartoons for children, specially com-
missioned by BBC television.

JERZY KOTOWSKI

The following three films represent Kotowski's extremely wide range of experimental techniques.

The Musical Box
(Poland, 1969)

The strong tradition of Polish puppet-making lies behind the contemporary figure-design in this film.

JERZY KOTOWSKI

The World in Opera
(Poland, 1969)

A combination of three-dimensional object animation and schematized graphic design.

Shadow of Time
(Poland, 1969)

Three-dimensional objects are used to make a dramatic statement in this anti-war film.

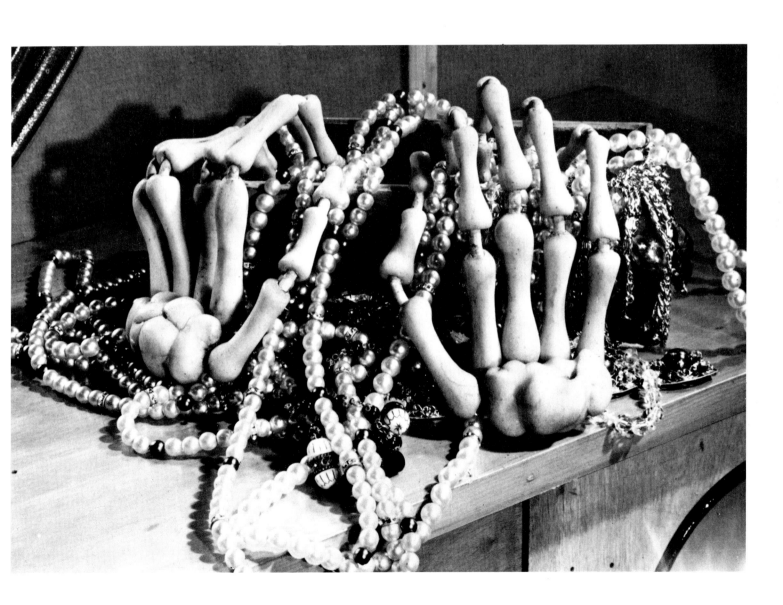

ALEKSANDAR MARKS
VLADIMIR JUTRIŚA

Sisyphus
(Yugoslavia, 1969)

Ranko Munitić writes that this film 'presents an introverted man, weighed down in the prison of his apartment: it seems that time has stayed still in the musty room, and that he is unable to start it. A strange séance takes place; parts of the furniture and fittings revolt against this state of things—drawers, chests and doors begin to fight against the lethargy of their master. Forced into action, the man destroys the things around him and, finally, remains quite alone in his room, confronted by the absurdity which had been hidden, not in the things, but in himself.'

Munitić adds that *Sisyphus* represents 'the eternal conflict between worlds and epochs in the human mind, the defeat of the burdened spirit which vanishes slowly in its own absurdity and loses the most important battle, the battle for dignity of personality and for creative affirmation in the surrounding world'.

ELEKTRA STUDIOS

Designers: Bob Blechman
            Harry Fernandez
            Dolores Cannata
            William Steig

Television commercials provide an excellent
medium in which to try out new trends in
graphic design, such as the influence of
pop art and other stylized graphic forms.

Puma Soft Drink
(USA, 1969)

Puma Soft Drink
(USA, 1969)

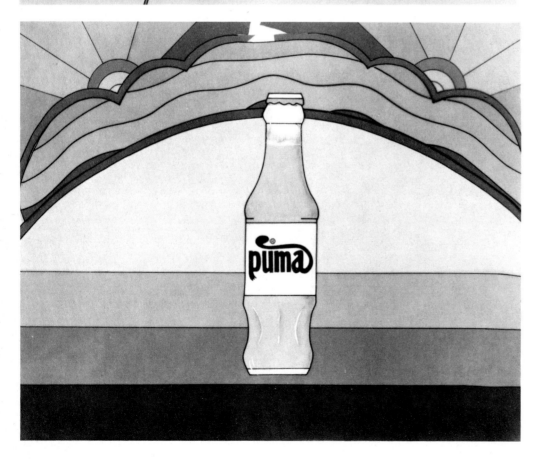

Pan Am Clipper Cargo *How's Business?*
(USA, 1969)

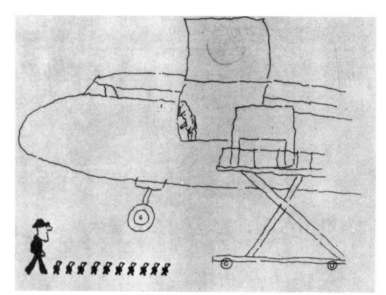

Pan Am helps your business take off

132

Sergeant's Sentry Dog Collar *Flee-Proof Dog*
(USA, 1969)

Alka Seltzer *Stomach Talk*
(USA, 1969)

Nervine *Bundle of Nerves*
(USA, 1969)

BELVISION

Tintin and the Sun-Temple
(Belgium, 1969)

This feature film is based on the book of the same title by the Belgian cartoonist, Hergé. The studio has specialized more recently in feature-length cartoons sponsored by Belgian Television.

ANTE ZANINOVIC

Of Holes and Corks
(Yugoslavia, 1968)

This fable concerns a man who shuts himself off from the world in a castle: when a mysterious power emanates from the earth he tries desperately to block its entrance through the nooks and crannies of the building, though he is prepared merely to play with the sounds the power produces. The final destruction of the building points to the defeat of a limited neutrality.

ZDENEK MILER

The Velvet Caterpillar
(Czechoslovakia, 1967)

A pleasantly designed entertaining film for children.

MIROSLAW KIJOWICZ

Panopticum
(Poland, 1969)

Another example showing the effectiveness of simplicity of design.

JOY BATCHELOR

The Five
(Great Britain, 1970)

This film was made to promote foot care, but the style reflects the subject through abstract forms. The toes are symbolized in a schematic design and, from time to time under stress, are shown as real characters. The appeal is made primarily through the emotions to the audience for whom this film was made, girls aged 13 to 15.

BORIVOJ DOVNIKOVIC

Krek
(Yugoslavia, 1968)

Krek is about a poet whose only freedom from his dread of compulsion, dogma and puritan stupidity, is obtained through dreams.

GIULIO GIANINI
DEANNA WISBEY

The Garden
(Britain/Italy, 1970)

The subject of this film was inspired by the story of Adam and Eve.

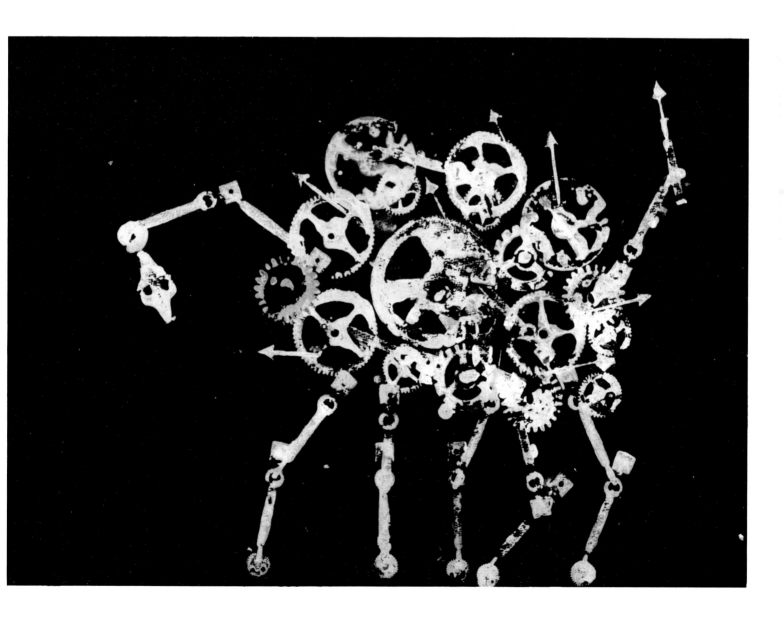

ZLATKO GRGIC

Invention of Shoes
(Yugoslavia, 1967)

This film tells the story of an ingenious scientist who decides to
produce shoes instead of bombs.

NEDELJKO DRAGIĆ

The Passing Days
(Yugoslavia, 1968)

A partially surrealist film in its subject and treatment, *The Passing Days* has some affinities with British Goon fantasy, but its speed is characteristic of American humour.

Diogenes Perhaps
(Yugoslavia, 1968)

A wanderer searches in vain for a being similar to himself and in the process misses the opportunity to pass through a door leading to a world of greater, more intense reality.

Diogenes Perhaps

FRANTISEK VYSTRCIL

Kosmodrom—Year 1999
(Czechoslovakia, 1969)

A bold graphic style creates a humorous and imaginative tale of the future. Both style and story are influenced by the work of Jan Brdecka.

DON ARIOLI

The House that Jack Built
(Canada, 1968)

There is a fluidity of motion in this film, a free flow of graphic line, combined with inventive visual ideas.

VATROSLAV MIMICA
ALEKSANDAR MARKS

The Fly
(Yugoslavia, 1967)

A dramatic film in both graphic style and subject. A fly assumes human dimensions while a man shrinks to the size of a fly.

JOSEF KABRT

The Nightingale and the Rose
(Czechoslovakia, 1968)

A story based on Oscar Wilde's fairy tale and inspired by Aubrey Beardsley's graphic style.

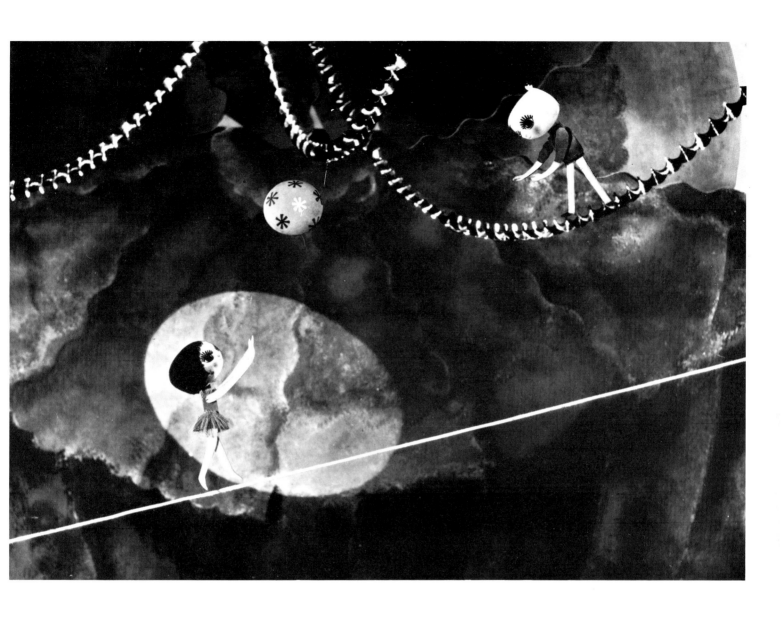

KATJA GEORGI
HEINRICH-GREIF-PREISTRAGER

Der Gardinentraum
(East Germany, 1969)

This film comes from a studio which has been moving towards more contemporary forms of design: three-dimensional objects are animated against a decorative graphic background.

MIKE MILLS

Tax is not a Four Letter Word
(Canada, 1969)

The strength of this film lies in the details of its visual treatment
rather than in its graphic design as a whole.

148

In a Box
(Canada, 1969)

A very economical use is made in this film of simplified line drawing.

King Size
(Canada, 1969)

A propaganda film against smoking.

IVAN RENC
PAVEL HOBBL
FRANTISEK BRAUN

The Black Magician
(Czechoslovakia, 1969)

The film uses a simplified realism; some sections of the film turn into surrealistic compositions.

IVAN RENC
MIROSLAV STEPANEK

The Sword
(Czechoslovakia, 1968)

The sword is used as the dominant object in the film on which the grotesque animated cartoon characters move. A satiric story with a sharp edge to its conclusion.

NIKOLA MAJDAK
BORISLAV ŠAJTINAC

The Spring of Life
(Yugoslavia, 1969)

The story of the film derives from the biblical legend of the spring
of life, which cures the sick and the lame, while the graphic treatment
is a development from the work of Kristifor Zefarouvc, a Siberian
artist of the eighteenth century.

ROBERT STENHOUSE

(New Zealand, 1969)

Designs from an introductory sequence to a religious programme (1), and a short film in a children's religious programme (2, 3, 4).

New Zealand is developing animation on a relatively small scale under the sponsorship of television.

3

4

In the Beginning

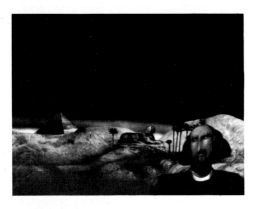  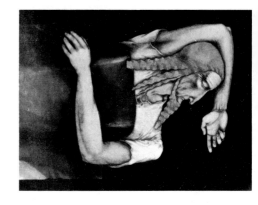

The Owl and the Pussycat

V. RADILOVICH
M. ANTERI

Commercial for 'Samson Wine'
(Venezuela, 1970)

These are the first films to be produced by a new team of international artists (from Italy, Yugoslavia, Spain and Peru), based in Venezuela.

V. RADILOVICH
E. MUNDO

It's Time to go to Bed
(Venezuela, 1970)

(opposite top)
PAUL BIRKBECK and
GRAHAM McCULLAM (designers)

In the Beginning
(Great Britain, 1970)

A series of 12 stories by BBC television, based on the Old Testament. A minimum of conventional cell animation was used, most of the movement being achieved by the movement of the rostrum camera and special optical effects.

(opposite below)
HILARY HAYTON

The Owl and the Pussycat
(Great Britain, 1969)

A short cartoon for children produced for BBC television.

R. O. BLECHMAN
AL KOUZEL

The Emperor's New Armor
(USA, 1969)

R. O. Blechman is one of the leading cartoonists in the United States, his work being published in many journals and advertising campaigns. His contribution to animation dates back to U.P.A. during the 1950s. In this film, made in collaboration with Al Kouzel, and based on his book, he uses his familiar style achieving a maximum effect with a minimum of graphic line. He is a cartoonist whose pointed humour depends on a graphic sharpness. In the background he introduces pastel colours to emphasize his bold use of black and white characters.

ISTVAN IMRE

Bill has a Hundred Faces
(Hungary, 1969)

A modernized form of three-dimensional
object animation, technically well executed.

ATTILA DARGAY

Variations on a Dragon
(Hungary, 1969)

Although the characters are designed tradi-
tionally, the film itself is full of visual ideas
and shows a fresh approach to story
development.

JOSZEF NEPP

Five Minutes Thrill
(Hungary, 1967)

This film which contains a chain of amusing gags performed by roughly-sketched characters, retains the freshness of improvised penmanship.

JOSEF GEMES

Koncertissimo
(Hungary, 1968)

A richness of textural design is excellently combined with comic ideas.

ETIEN RAIK

14 Juillet à Nutsville
(France, 1969)

An example of object animation, using nuts and nutcrackers as characters. The 'legs' of each nutcracker were drilled and a needle screwed in at the base. By means of these needles the nutcrackers could be stuck in the base, which was made of cork.

The number of pictures corresponding to each bar of the music determines mathematically the time-motion relationship. But it is the sensitivity of the animator's fingers which determines the harmony of the movement, the flexibility in speeding up and slowing down.

This sensitivity is decisive in the target which the animation of objects sets for itself, which should be to avoid bestowing upon objects movements which imitate human beings.

VERA LINNECAR
NANCY HANNA

Television series for the General Post Office
(Great Britain, 1968-9)

A distinctive form of humour, combined with good design and filmic sense.

CURT LINDA

Conference of the Animals
(West Germany, 1969)

This full length animated film, based on a story by Erich Kartner,
is the work of the newly emerging German designers.

LASSE LINDBERG

For Rent
(Sweden, 1968)

Lindberg combines abstract graphics with realistic live images.

SABIN BALASA

Valul
(Roumania, 1969)

A film primarily composed of classical paintings, in which the movement is provided by means of smooth dissolves, tracks and pans.

RICHARD TAYLOR

Computers
(Great Britain, 1969)

Computers, directed by Peter de Normanville with animation by Richard Taylor, deals with man's relations to machines.

ESTUDIOS MACIAN

El Majo de los Gueños
(Spain, 1969)

This feature follows traditional lines of story
and design.

ESTUDIOS MACIAN

Biencil Mundial de la Histoneta
(Spain-Argentina, 1968)

The style, derived from the strip cartoon, achieves a highly dramatic effect by bold use of graphics.

GOLDSHOLL ASSOCIATES

TV commercial for Eastman Kodak Company
(USA, 1969)

Goldsholl Associates combine several techniques, such as cut-out,
live-action and superimposition, for this commercial. The integration
is most successful.

PIT FLICK
RUDIGER FUNKE

Mister X
(West Germany, 1969)

This opening, which combines simplified live action and quick object animation, conveys the dramatic flavour of the programme.

DAVID NEWTON (art director)

Anxiety: TV commercial for 'Book of Life'
(Great Britain, 1969)

In this visually surrealistic approach to the TV commercial, Newton basically uses live-action techniques, but the shots are composed in terms of graphic design.

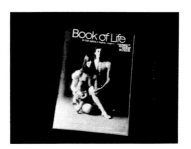

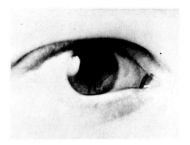

GAMMA FILMS

Langnese
(Italy, 1969)

Gamma Films' strength lies in their quality of design and colour.

Da Racconti di E. A. Poe
(Italy, 1969)

PAVLE STALTER
BRANKO RANITOVIC

Mask of the Red Death
(based on a story by E. A. Poe)
(Yugoslavia, 1969-70)

One of the most difficult tasks in animation is to make texturized figures move convincingly. Most attempts in the past have failed. This is because the textures of the figures have to be followed through in the consecutive phases of the movement, and the frame-by-frame changes satisfactorily integrated. The reason why the majority of animated pictures are conceived in simple outlined figures is explained by this difficulty.

The artists write: 'Made in collage technique, the film represents a new ''penetration'' by the Zagreb School into the field of animated paintings; Pavle Stalter, the principal designer of this film, was the designer of the backgrounds, animator and co-director—he has shown, an astonishing ability to animate complicated phenomena in the art of painting which, in certain instances, may well be equal to any achievements of classical painting.'

ALAN COOPER
P. MONKCOM

TV commercial for Dot lavatory cleaner
(Great Britain, 1969)

A good example of the influence of kinetic art on the cinematic treatment of everyday objects for the purpose of promoting consumer goods.

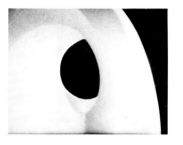 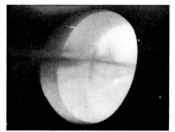  

 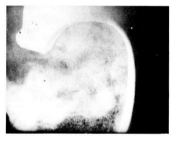  

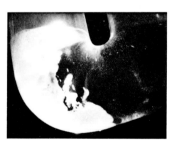 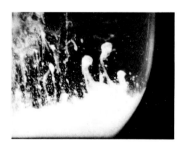  

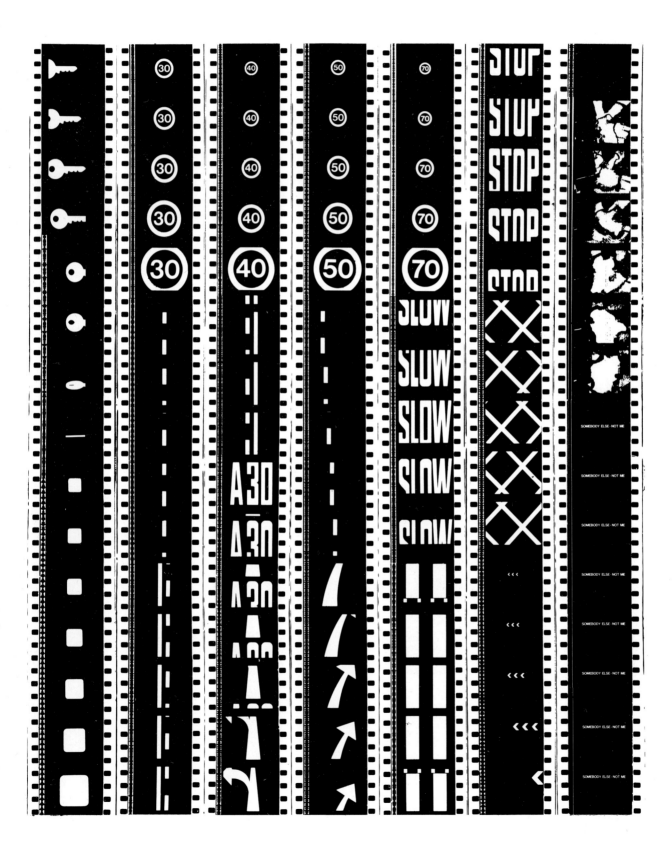

178

STEFAN PSTROWSKI (designer)

Somebody Else Not Me
(Great Britain, 1969)

The Education Programme
(Great Britain, 1970)

John Stamp of Moreno Cartoons produced this thirty-second promotion film for a Thames Television 'report' documentary on the subject of 'madness on the roads'.

Main title sequence for a programme about trends in education by BBC television.

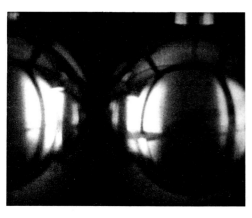

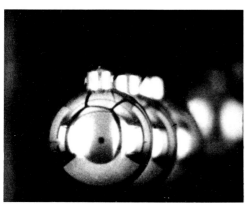

PETER CLARK

Children's programme for Granada Television
(Great Britain, 1969)

Clark uses a combination of geometrical forms and cut-outs for this programme opening. The fast moving visual changes make an exciting beginning.

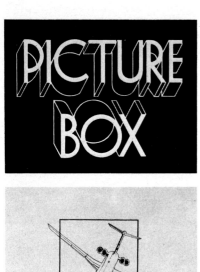
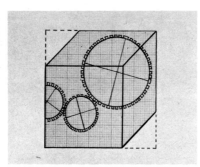
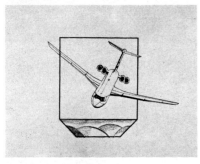
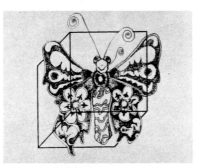

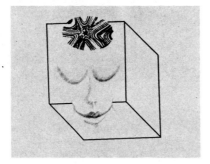

4 Speculation

Since the opportunities for communication between artists of various territories are frequent, and since the number of recognized colleges and universities where the art of animation is being taught is increasing, it is clear that some considerable advances should take place. In the future, however, animation is bound to have a far wider range of meaning for audiences as well as artists. Activities will range from cartoons to longer dramatic features, from short teaching films to complex computer-processed scientific films, from abstract experimental avant-garde films to large-scale kinetic happenings; conceptions will be carried out on flat surfaces as well as on mobile screens, executed free hand as well as with the aid of small scale computers, programmed instantly at home and conveyed to a central processing machine for the final output. The content too will become more sophisticated. These changes will create a new and more discriminating audience, accepting films with higher and more demanding values in design and intellectual content.

The film is a medium in which 'art for art's sake' is always possible; it can be totally self-indulgent if its makers want it to be so. But its strength lies in the fact that it can also be useful. It is used effectively in a wide range of communication, from advertising to scientific instruction, from entertainment to avant-garde experiment. The need to solve problems in the advertising and sponsored film has stimulated new approaches in film continuity and editing techniques. The new optical, special effects service, for instance, emerged in consequence of demands by the advertising industry for television commercials. So did the style of visual continuity, a rhythmical advance which means that a thirty-second commercial can include 30 to 40 shots instead of 5 to 10, which was normal some years ago.

Since the new visual vocabulary of film language is being enriched by such fundamental new provisions as the computer and holography, as well as by other kinds of electronically processed pictures and the whole range of new optical effects achieved either with new lenses or the rostrum camera, one must assume that the areas of their utilization will similarly be enlarged, especially in the fields of education and technical instruction. Expansion will also take place in the advertising film and film as a free art form.

In education, we have already experienced a dramatic breakthrough in films specially designed for the classroom. The spread of 8-mm cassette-loaded film loops in Western Europe and the United States points the way ahead. These specially-made teaching films are now used as a normal aid to teaching in the classroom, clarifying and fortifying by visual means chemistry, biology, physics and mathematics, making facts and processes more easy to memorize than the old methods which relied on text book illustration and the blackboard.

Film is particularly useful for describing processes which cannot be easily demonstrated in the classroom, for example, how a molecule chain is actually bonded, how the ear actually works, how a plant actually grows, or the relationship between force, mass and motion. So far, however, its potentialities have only just begun to be exploited. Conservative teachers still resist breaking away from the printed word. It is likely, however, that a combination of the two, text working alongside mobile visual illustration by means of film, will finally emerge as standard practice in teaching and there will be a great opportunity for the film-maker to produce his individual contribution. At the same time we must hope that the visual material he creates will contain new ideas, and will be produced in a form which is able to influence the students to appreciate good design.

There has been a similar development in the production of information films for industrial and government organizations. Films, especially if they use animation, have a capacity to demonstrate the working method of an organization, its structure, even its policy, with economy, speed and clarity. The spectacular growth of 16-mm production in this field is indicative. Films are being produced by industry today for an exceptionally wide range of purposes. For example, in demonstrating the exact function of a new tool, the combination of animation, to demonstrate the inner structure of the mechanism, with live action, to show its actual appearance and observable functioning, has become the normal approach. But with the introduction of new optical techniques, this more obvious division of presentation can be broken down, and something quite new offered. For instruction in new methods of management and the use of computers, for instructing apprentices, nurses, doctors, pilots, and literally hundreds of other professionals, young or not so young, film has become the accepted medium. The majority of the films produced for these purposes, however, do not even approach their potential. An entirely new point of view is needed in the technique and the treatment of the subject matter of these films, whether they are produced on modest or generous budgets.

The wholly didactic approach which is so often used does not catch the attention of the audience, who seem to be stimulated only by the quick-firing style of television. Instructional films, no matter how dull the subject may appear to be, can be made stimulating by adopting an inductive approach, which offers the audience closer personal participation in what they are seeing on the screen. An imaginative use of graphic design, instead of the customary superficial 'documentary' approach of the live-action film, can at once make a picture more interesting.

The range of new electronic techniques, especially the computer-graphical approach, can establish a new era in this branch of film-making. The subject must be *penetrated*, to reveal some of the achievements of research which are impossible to show by mere surface demonstration or verbal explanation. Production methods can be recorded as a blue print, so that the scientist can create his own films in a matter of days instead of months, using the various electronic systems available.

Opportunities in the advertising industry have never been greater than they will be in the 1970s. Advertising has always been quick to utilize new visual ideas, and even acts as a catalyst to technical invention. Many of the new technical ideas described here were first seen by the general public in television commercials. It is interesting to note that advertising is no longer confined to capitalist countries, but is currently used in nations with tightly controlled economies, such as Russia, Czechoslovakia, Roumania and Hungary, while it was introduced into Yugoslavia some time ago. In fact, wherever consumer goods have to be moved from manufacturer to customer, the mass medium of film is used to inform the public. The manner of persuasion can, however, differ vastly from the dynamic appeal of 'hard sell' to the gentler efforts of persuasion, or 'soft sell'. In most eastern European countries, the 'soft sell' approach is preferred. The main difference in the approach to advertising in the East, however, is not so much in the nature of the subject-matter, as in its time-scale. Unlike the normal twenty to thirty second limit in the West, anything between two to five minutes is allowed to explain the advantages of some consumer article.

More than any other category of film, the advertising film cuts across the barriers which exist between live action, animation and special effects techniques, often using all three within a matter of seconds. A small proportion of the many thousands of television commercials made create something novel, something which may have been tried out first on short experimental and art films. This novelty alone can lead to television commercials becoming among the most imaginative achievements of television film-making. Abstract or semi-abstract animation, stop-motion object animation, photo animation, strobe effects, optical superimposition of live action and cartoon, aerial image combination effects, have all appeared many times on the television screen in an attempt to persuade the public, either coolly or emotionally, to buy the product advertised. The vocabulary of visual 'tricks' is constantly expanding, and where these stop, the techniques of the laboratory can offer new visual solutions. It is the responsibility of the advertising agency's art director and his creative department, as well as the clients', to decide how these new technical facilities can best be used.

In spite of the great advances in film graphics, it is the animated feature film which lags furthest behind in the use of new techniques. This is not because of any lack of production—just the opposite. During the early 1970s no less than twenty feature-length animated films were being produced around the world, while a large number of live-action features use animated graphics for their credit titles. This figure must be compared with the one or two films produced every year over the last two decades.

It would appear that the live-action production and exhibition industry is satisfied to change the size of the cinema screen and the size of the film negative in order to achieve a larger picture on the screen, and is under the illusion that as a result the medium has been revolutionized. Yet the visual style and conventions used for wide-screen in the films so far produced remain the same as they were thirty years ago. In fact, in the majority of cases there is less visual awareness and filmcraft, if one considers the standard of visual composition in the films of Eisenstein, Carl Dreyer, or even the early Keaton films, which used techniques of montage, split-screen and rhythmical continuity. The relationship of form to content is an area which still needs to be worked out in the feature film. When the relationship between size and content in pictorial composition, and the use of sound along with an interesting storyline, is brought into harmony as it was in the film *2001—A Space Odyssey* or, to some extent, in *The Yellow Submarine*, the final result can be very rewarding. The spacious image possible with 65-mm negative and 70-mm positive film blown up on the screen to dimensions such as 120 by 50 feet, certainly offers a challenge to the visualizer, which so far has seldom been properly developed. The giant cinerama lenses can magnify actuality magnificently, but they are blind to anything which lies beyond mere realism. When graphic invention extends into this field, using contemporary cinematographic techniques, the claims made for the 'spectacular' in the cinema will at last be genuinely realized. More especially, the possibilities of visual magnetic tape, monitored electronically for the manipulation of colours ranging from the realistic to the abstract, are going to repay exploration. Similarly, certain shapes can be segmented and filled with abstract tonal compositions, while abstract forms can be juxtaposed with realistic backgrounds, or vice versa. Recording by the television camera through electronic monitors can provide a range of effects which reproduction by means of the live-action optical camera has not yet achieved. The combination of the two systems can obviously enrich the film director's visual vocabulary. However, such developments as these lie ahead. Eventually a system will be evolved enabling the cameras to be operated by computers, with the electronic effects integrated with the camera's image on specially coated magnetic material. This will replace the present bromide film base, so saving the whole laboratory reproductive processes. The visuals will be played back after preparing a master tape, from which master copies can be made for immediate release to the cinemas. Apart from producing a final product of a far superior quality, this process would have the advantage of allowing for a much higher degree of concentration on the artistic content of the film in the production team. Films could be made more economically, because many of the most troublesome areas of film production would be avoided—processes such as developing and printing the film stock.

In conclusion, the most advanced visual invention is likely to continue to be found in short films in the experimental and avant-garde class. So far activity in these areas has been confined to films made by hand, using such novel techniques as scratching on the emulsion of filmstock or painting directly on film. From now on, however, techniques resulting from the use of digital and the various analogue computers will be available to the experimentalists. The interest in the medium shown by painters such as d'Avino and Bourak is having a direct influence on the non-technical area of film-making, bringing animation much nearer to the plastic arts. Fortunately, the boundaries are melting between the classical approach in film craft and a freer expression using a far wider range of integrated visual possibilities. The sharp division between cartoon figures with hard outlines and figures with outlines which merge more fluidly with their backgrounds no longer exists: the choice is open to the artist. Similarly with the sharp division which has existed between the animated film and live action. These conventional divisions have persisted since the beginning of film. Modern technology and creative thinking need no longer accept such limitations. The aerial image system of photography and the new range of optical effects, as well as the entirely fresh conception of film-making evolved by certain of the younger generation of film-makers and graphic artists, are gradually establishing a form of film-making which lies somewhere in between animation and the actuality of live-action photography; it makes use of both, but treats photography as a starting point only. The graphic conception begins, therefore, with photography as a technique, but live characters and real backgrounds can be introduced with a sense of graphic organization unrestricted by gravity or any of the other limitations in formal relationships usually inherent in live-action treatment. The new techniques must also include holography, if it is mastered by the artist and used with imagination. Holography could make a substantial contribution in the world of television, cinema and the fine arts, bringing them much closer together.

If a study were to be made of the outstanding achievements in the cinema, it would soon become clear that the great majority of good films owe more to the imagination than to technical achievement. A further study would also make it clear that films of this kind are usually based on some newly developed methods of film-making initiated by an individual rather than on the inventions of some research department. Such were the early films of Disney and McLaren. Although the film itself is a scientific invention, depending on a number of interlocking developments in mechanics, as a recording instrument it is in itself sterile. It depends for its progress on imagination, creative insight, and the constructive application of relevant aesthetic values. These can be developed much more readily by individuals working in the freer atmosphere of short film production, without commercial pressures and compromise. Nevertheless, the main enterprise of the world film industry is concentrated on the production of commercial features, together with television and cinema advertising films.

It is also obvious that the audience of today, influenced by television and space research, is very different from the audience of a few years ago. Most films produced a decade ago have little current impact. The stimulus of contemporary film is being developed on a different plane, especially in the speed of visual presentation. A more complete understanding of the function of perception would assist us in achieving these new qualities in film-making. A more detailed analysis of human reaction is necessary, and will be much more so in the future, following the introduction of the new techniques and ideas we have suggested. Similarly, a new kind of artist and film-maker will be needed, who is able to communicate on an appropriate level with the new generations of audience: he will be familiar with contemporary techniques of science and will have made a study of audience psychology. Most important, he will also be prepared to take advantage of the new opportunities which are being opened up to fulfil the ever-expanding needs of our visual imagination.

Actual standard sizes of 8- to 65-mm
negative film

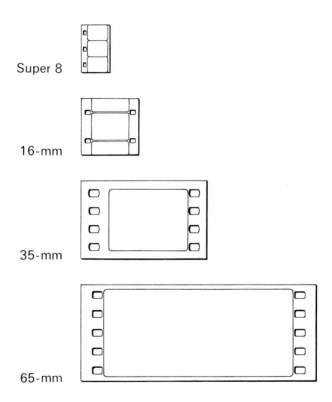

Super 8

16-mm

35-mm

65-mm

A schematic analysis of the relationship between kinetic art and animated film

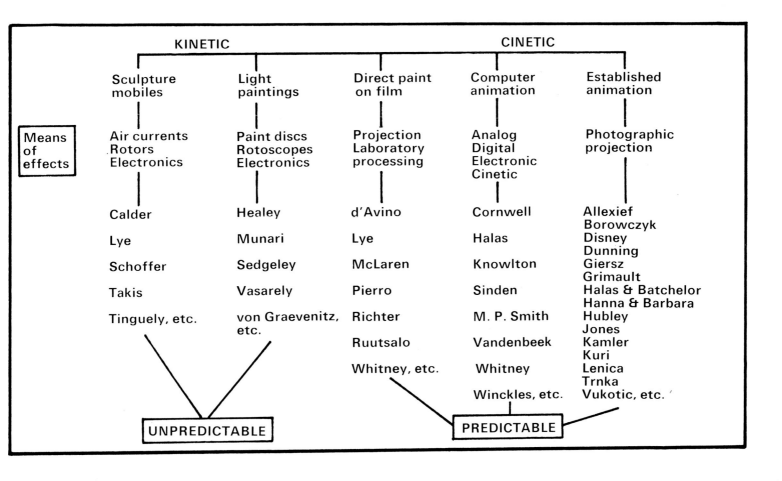

Index